SERIE d'ECRITURE
No. 13/14

CROSSCUT UNIVERSE

Writing on Writing
from France

Edited and Translated by Norma Cole

BURNING DECK, PROVIDENCE
2000

SERIE d'ECRITURE is an annual of current French writing in English translation. The first five issues were published by SPECTACULAR DISEASES, which continues to be the sole source for European distribution and subscription. Since No. 6, the publisher has been Burning Deck in Providence, RI.
Editor: Rosmarie Waldrop

Individual copies $10. Subscription for 2 issues: $16.
Supplements: $5.
In England: £5. 2 issues: £8. Postage 25p/copy.
Distributors:
Small Press Distribution, 1341 Seventh St,. Berkeley CA 94710
1-800/869-7553; orders@spdbooks.org
Spectacular Diseases, c/o Paul Green, 83b London Rd., Peterborough, Cambs. PE2 9BS
US subscriptions only: Burning Deck, 71 Elmgrove Ave., Providence RI 02906

Versions of some texts were first published in the magazines *Exile: The Literary Quarterly* (2000), *Série d'Ecriture* (1993), *Two Lines* (2000), *Tyuonyi* ("Violence of the White Page: Contemporary French Poetry," 1991) and in the following chapbooks: Anne-Marie Albiach, *A Discursive Space* (Sausalito, CA: Duration Press, 1999); Emmanuel Hocquard, *This Story is Mine* (Saratoga, CA: Instress, 1999).

Cet ouvrage, publié dans le cadre d'un programme d'aide à la publication, bénéficie du soutien du Ministère des Affaires Etrangères et du Service Culturel de l'Ambassade de France aux Etats-Unis.
This work, published as part of a program of aid for publication, received support from the French Ministry of Foreign Affairs and the Cultural Services of the French Embassy in the United States.

Burning Deck is the literature program of Anyart: Contemporary Arts Center, a tax-exempt non-profit corporation.

ISSN 0269-0179
ISBN 1-886224-39-0

Cover art by Raquel

CROSSCUT UNIVERSE

CONTENTS

"Par ces rappels, je n'entends rien prouver, mais seulement orienter l'attention."
—Maurice Blanchot, *L'entretien infini*

There are conversations embedded in these pages, a kind of cross-talk through time and space. Texts, interviews, critical pieces, journal entries, letters, worknotes and at least one simple list make visible and audible an openwork of embodied voices in conversation, in the deliberate breaking open of intentionalities, isolating single elements at one extremity, multiple folds, complex rhythmic architectonics in the process of being constructed and deconstructed at the other. Most of these pieces have been published in France in literary journals, as books or as parts of books, although at least one has been circulated privately as a "report." One text, a guest become ghost, was revoked when the author, although pleased with the translation, decided his own text needed to be completely rewritten. Some of the writing here will extend the available work of writers previously translated and now familiar to North American readers, while a number of texts will introduce new work and new names.

Dialogic threads echo and reverberate through considerations of body and book, silence as both restraint and production of meaning, the neuter or neutral as the unassigned in relation to sociopolitical complexities of address, the sentence of syntax and precedent. Sets of references indicate points of orientation and question assumptions of assignment. Their generosity and hospitality are striking as is their rigor of investigation. Writing is action, the phenomenological self entering language, already a specific set of conditions within conditions. Writing and its silences are made up of specific concrete decisions. Circumstances and events (such as two world wars and the Algerian struggle for independence), from detail to detail, date to date, are not backdrop but determining facts appearing at different focal lengths, from naming to silence, testing the orders of apprehension as well as of writing.

Here is a range of writing at varying stages of coming into being, self-aware, proposing a stance very different from the taxonomy of "text/paratext." In *Beginnings*, Edward Said asserts, "One of the critical distinctions of modern literature is the importance given by the writer to his own paratexts — writings that explore his working problems in making a text." The opposite impulse is at work here, for what is of interest is how the texts read together intentionally or inadvertently, addressing each other and writing beyond the limits of this or any single volume.

Norma Cole

Anne-Marie Albiach

Letter to Jean Daive
[October 1968]

Dear Jean,

I tell you as echo. from the very edges from where already you answer back.

I am "touched." I was going to use the masculine form, to neutralize, but will not let myself succumb to such word play, un-pleasant and un-worthy of our situation of mutuality — and no doubt, ambiguity — sensitive to evasion. clarification. (study).

I am answering you — too quickly —. I speak from beyond the present act...but.

I would like to make clear my use of "mental" — physical, organic, phonic chemistry — *above all structure* — and it is this structure I seek — ready to locate the dismemberment at the very center of rigor and of vigor of the paths.

The structure is spiral: at least, seen in perspective — not in its volume — perspective it takes upon a blank sheet of paper. the impulse is spiral impulse. if the spiral coincides with itself. we remain in this new illusory of perceptions — in the circle keeping us vertical, preventing our "falling on the very luxuri- ousness of the paving stones" — (premonitory vertical).

---

fig., No. 3 (1990)

This vertical inhabits our "nape." in fact we believe we walk horizontally. absent from time. speechless from movement.

Pleasure and defeat, if ripping of the spiral which relocates itself, which opens itself. inverse procedures: breath no breath. initial verb, initiatory perpetuated breath, the word made movement — (flesh) — the spiral sometimes does not spare us and so the circle disappears, volume is seen

(volume)

which for me would be of "mental" tenor. syntactic structure. non-given of impulse by the non-stopping of elocution of movement. into these circular places of appearances, reincarnated but impassible are placed memory, retrospective, affectivity, *vision*, speech, absence

what you call persiflage
  "waiting
for our steps on the
  gravel"

is the persiflage of opening: persif lage being that decadence of volume inhaled or exhaled in the breath. the language that corresponds to those structures does not seem to be that of the subtraction in addition. that which resists the name. the concept. which eludes the verb. which magnifies the subject to the state of the object. circulatory language positive-negative as far as its LOCUTION: of, by, while, by which, ad-verb, position placing me on the dizzy extremity of the curve. no longer about writing — almost. But writing is its THEME.

All that would not exist without writing which persists. the "said" (graphic dance of the breath. movement) pre-exists perhaps, and the propelling gesture equally, I would have it.

I do not think a system possible: mechanical. baroque. are apparent or real. but secondary. it allows me of itself, to be. if not, there is no writing. the system calls itself endowed with breath (locutory). if not, it is not. not even system.

I am not defending myself, I am trying — very very partially — to clarify — the ripping in the act of writing is located between impulse and the impulse that wants to be systematized with writing's safety in mind. this stage passed, returns the absence of the verb, volume's reflection. that said, I do not *believe* anything. nor think. I would like to speak of you. I have "killed" you in my poem. by necessity of the volume, precisely. I will not do it just now. for want of a *blank*: space of memory.

END: I am very moved by that letter — "violent" — finally from you. I should like to know even more. you are right to clarify those abysses: "there, on the left." and I follow you there...

In all friendship —

Anne-Marie Albiach

Anne-Marie Albiach

A Letter & a Text for Jean Tortel

Paris, 17-5-69

Dear Jean Tortel,

You are not unaware of how difficult it is to "speak." About RELATIONS — knowing full well the relative poverty of any approach, the presence of language as material, and its abstraction often confuse me.

For a long time I have hesitated to send you this text in which I try, rather than to show, to suggest the attraction — and the hesitancies at times — that your "project" has roused in me. I hope you will read it "warmly," I mean, discovering beyond the words and syntax the risks I take to follow you.

My best wishes,
Anne-Marie A.

After LES VILLES OUVERTES, Jean Tortel published RELATIONS with Gallimard. Composed of "Liminaire," "Frontières d'un espace," "Phrases pour un orage," "Critique d'un Jardin," "Explications de textes," "Gestes de la Marquise," and, finally, "Critique d'un language," — last phase of the book from which *l'Ephémère* has just published excerpts — the naming of these parts can be considered explicatory: the mental setting, of peaceful ambiguity, seems to preexist for Jean Tortel in spite of this structure, abrupt but of contemplative speech.

Most certainly, Hérodiade's shadow declares those erudite cascades of syntax where writing falls back on itself and takes itself as subject; unexpected syntax with verbs whose object,

Action Poétique, No. 99 (1985)

unhoped for — or hopeless — emerges into the most unsuspected *virgin* equilibrium. One might perhaps think that this blueprint of the absence between the subject and the "spoken" or the verb, precedes us in a veritable lack, and not uniquely in an experienced opening. This uncertainty remains even in the face of the semblance of quietudes about which Philippe Jacottet himself could be mistaken.... Such uncertainty would come from a commitment not to withdraw from the adjective in its immoderate use.

From his "allées" toward the earth, that of the garden to be precise, enclosed earth of enclosed space, Jean Tortel sometimes keeps the illicit correlation of cause to effect, and forgets to consider the tool (of gardening) as isolated in itself but believes in its effectiveness. Likewise with language, which he does not, however, stop isolating and exposes to us in its simple birth, *writing born from writing* in "Explications de textes," or born of culture with "Gestes de la Marquise." Considering "Explications de textes," discomfort, it seems, is unavoidable: the first texts, submitted as theme — or territory — carry within them givens that would doubtless have the power of platitude such as Francis Ponge, in a displacement of the sense of time, achieves today.... It would seem that Jean Tortel betrays his purpose, prescribing poems too brilliant that would remain only subtitles inducing a certain nostalgia for their source. Of course it is not systematic that writing gives birth to writing, and that metamorphosis necessitates a wholly other awakening than that of skill or of the absence of the subject, a serious game, difficult to submit to its own chance.

Ambiguity, meanwhile, remains alive, which astonishes in the available research of the poet; he does not cease, at the risk of returning to the neutrality of gesture, to absent himself from the evasion of colors, scents, figures, that hold on, let go.

Brilliant, finally, the Marquise could be Hérodiade or as easily Madame Edwarda: the cruelty of the "I" appears in the eroticism of her "outings," where, rather than in fiction, Jean Tortel places his trust in doubtful time "regarding the dead marquise." A dramatization that Bataille would not deny.

Anne-Marie Albiach/Jean Daive

A Discursive, Space

Paris, 22 July 1978

Jean Daive: What gives this impression of somnolence?

Anne-Marie Albiach: I think Beckett tried to suppress social and visible corporeity and above all to bind it to the object. There is a kind of will to simplify the body in the event it bears. In *First Love* this is expressed very distinctly. For example, he expresses his way...you spoke of somnolence, and for him sleep is without doubt very important since he refuses to let the body arrive at a level of wakefulness and he protects himself from wakefulness by sleeping with his clothes on, or keeping his hat on. The clothes are in no way symbolic. They are simply objects, objects that consume the body. In fact there is a permanent refusal of any integration, whatever it be...of the relation of the one with the other. Dialogue is impossible and if there is dialogue as in *First Love* it's a ridiculous dialogue. Besides ...the very title chosen for *First Love*, with all its tender implications, and the absolutely despairing text, may I say, of the non-relation of these two beings who meet gratuitously and live off prostitution, make Beckett take refuge in the greatest possible darkness...whether from society or from excrement, what comes out of the body. He throws into question all the evidence surrounding us: systems, the construction of houses, furniture. When he arrives and begins to live with his lover in *First Love,* he hastens to remove the furniture from the bedroom and to lie down without actually undressing, to doze in a semi-

FIN, No. 1 (1999)

sleep that fills his days. So there is a refusal to participate in active life and not only in active life but in the least motion. Communication takes place in waste.

*

A-M A: *First Love* has two different sites, a bench and a house. Then the character leaves at the birth of his son. He leaves simply because his son "leps" and he doesn't "lep."(*Laughs.*) So his son is superfluous. He would even disrupt the order of things.

JD: But from the beginning of the book there is a father problem.

A-M A: Yes...And there, something akin to tenderness must be noted. The father, that's still the Law. One law is accepted here, hierarchical. From his father he received permission to live...in this permanent withdrawal. The father protects him from others. The father is complicit. And in death the father has become an object. And once the father dies, the other members of the household send him away. Against the orders of the father who had stipulated that the character keep his room and way of life. But once the father is dead, he is thrown out. And he finds himself in the town he will denounce.

*

A-M A: *The Lost Ones* evokes a metamorphosis and instead of taking a character or two characters it embraces an entire situation. It calls up a whole sculptural construction of a cylinder that would enclose its characters within their destiny. The destiny of its characters — their life and death — is bound to very precise laws which are represented in the form of objects such as ladders. These objects are imperfect and cruel. The world is seen as an aggressive world, the world of objects. The ladders, for instance, do not really help someone who wants to go up to the top of the cylinder since there are always rungs missing, and the reader understands that someone who wants to go up is forced to come back down, and that there is nothing up there. While those who

17

stay below hope, he calls them "the sedentary," they have not moved. In a way, they are the winners, the ones who remain in that somnolence you spoke of. And the winners are losing their vision but have not been fooled and did not use a ladder to try to reach a fictive summit. Whatever has to do with birth or giving birth among the sedentary must be noted. The description, quite labored, of a woman and her child, a red-head whose hair falls across her face, who holds her child close, both of them in the state of wasting away "without noticing," emphasizes Beckett. And the sedentary around that woman and that child, who lift her hair off her face, indicating that there is still a kind of communication among the sedentary, half asleep and losing their vision. He goes so far as to specify that blue eyes, being more sensitive, lose their vision more quickly than the others. No detail escapes him in this elaboration of a metamorphosis.

JD: Is there a demolition of language that would occur from using two languages?

A-M A: Yes. There is a permanent counterpoint, that is, brightness-darkness. Day, night. While he passes indiscriminately from day to night, in his writing there is day and night. Which is additional ridicule, since it is to be understood at the second degree. Can I really believe he appreciates the scent of a garden? I think you have to read it at the second degree in his writing. In fact, his writing is open, while what he describes is closed.

JD: He has the good fortune to be manipulated by two languages.

*

Paris, 23 November 1990

JD: I would like to begin with the titles of two of your books, for instance the title of *État*, with its first letter in italic, which makes the title unpronounceable.

18

A-M A: Yes.

JD: So the title is first of all visual.

A-M A: It is visual.

JD: And the other title, *Mezza Voce*, which is vocal, musical.

A-M A: Yes. *Mezza Voce* says it well. The title is significant because it is true that there are excesses and they are protected by the title: *mezza voce*, with half voice. But I believe that in all of the texts that make up this book nothing is uttered mezza voce. I remember too that in another book I use a phrase in relation to a dialogue, "He spoke mezza voce," words were flowing in Italian.

JD: So État presents itself as a score.

A-M A: Yes. And again, *Mezza Voce* has a musical sense.

JD: But flattened, that is, the event-things occur on a stage.

A-M A: It's theatrical. It comes...and in État I even mention it, from Shakespeare, from my fascination with Shakespeare, and from *Macbeth* with the three witches. In État I speak of the female presences who utter the facts.

JD: How did you move from scoring (from what has to be made flat) to a theatrical stage, I mean where a play, something of a play, will take place? A play, and the characters, the subjects it requires.

A-M A: But there the subjects are, in short, Mallarméan. Fundamentally there is not that much difference between État and *Mezza Voce* except for the fact that État appears to be much more abstract. But the characters are determined by their pronouns: *he, she, they* feminine, *they* masculine. And movement is indicated in the text. I have shifted from theatrical abstraction to theatrical production.

19

JD: How are you able to distinguish the characters in *Mezza Voce*, the ones who whisper?

A-M A: The characters are anonymous. These characters are anonymous and it's this status that makes them powerful as I understand it. Because when I say "he"...to me, that's an anonymous character. I don't know exactly who he is. Or "she." I do not know exactly who she is.

JD: What energizes your theater? Does this theater support denouement or projection or the erasure of the pronominal subjects? What makes this kind of gravitational force or grand metabolics occur on that stage?

A-M A: It's lyricism. Because a lyric movement always attracts and repels its characters — anonymous — in their disappearance as well as in their presence. And they can be named within the text, named subjectively, objectively, for these characters sometimes become real characters. For instance I wrote a text "...Where the forest is darker" when my father died. But I don't articulate any form of the word father and I never articulate the word mother, my mother who was so present at the death of my father. So in fact even in the most extreme situations, like death, like a theme of death, like the death theme, the character remains anonymous. There is, let me say, affectivity that causes the anonymity to come and screen an emotion or a transgression.

JD: It isn't named because you are looking for the origin of characters, or Being, to account for its androgynous force and its energy.

A-M A: I don't think there is any real androgyny in *Mezza Voce*. In *Flammigère*, my first book, it was in question but — I think if I don't name it, it's to give it more power.

JD: The character?

A-M A: The character.

JD: What is androgyny...or the dream of androgyny?

A-M A: It is writing. It is writing which is at once male and female. I have never, with respect to myself, thought while writing that I was a woman. This may have been a shock to many women — but I do not write as a woman, I write as a writer, insofar as I am able to write. Which means that for me there is no difference between a text written...by a man or a text written by a woman. Contrary to what certain friends wanted to see, who thought they had to read *État* as a book written by a woman. When, for instance, I talk about the knife I think there has been an inappropriate analytic interpretation. If I mention a knife...it is for the pleasure of it. It was in Malraux's *The Human Condition*, I have never forgotten the first scene of the murder with the knife, but it becomes something else from the moment the character plunges the knife into his victim's body. And for me that is the knife in *État*, and I refuse to let anyone say "it's a woman's writing."

JD: Yet in *Mezza Voce* there is a whole set of properties which could eventually accrete to a woman's role, the female role.

A-M A: Yes, the ornaments, the jewelry...chains and other things that really do issue from a desire for theater.

JD: In order to critique it, or to ...

A-M A: No, to glorify it ...

JD: ...inventory...

A-M A: No...yes...I am very affected by ornament, by jewelry, by chains. But chains, they cut both ways. They are both ornaments and ornaments that take prisoners. And the curtains come from my real attraction, since adolescence, for the theater. I read a lot of theater. And the perfume, yes, perfume, chains, jewelry.

JD: *Mezza Voce* is constructed around grand theatrical moments. Perhaps not visible but which are so many points of reference in order to move the book along.

A-M A: I don't know quite how to answer. How would you rephrase that question?

JD: I'll ask the question differently.... For instance there are words like voice, theater, display, vocal dazzling and "yet," you write, "fiction has no more currency."

A-M A: Yes.

JD: So it did have currency?

A-M A: It had currency. But when I say "fiction has no more currency," it has its currency in saying "fiction has no more currency." This is the supreme fiction. When I articulate, when the writer articulates, "fiction has no more currency," it means that fiction is at its height.

JD: All right, I'll return to the previous question...was *Mezza Voce* created from a certain number of limit points of this fiction which has no more currency?

A-M A: Of course, yes. *Mezza Voce*, first of all, was not written quickly, but with texts that were a few years old. There is a continuity and I think that fiction is always present, not only fiction but Bataille's influence, with a certain disguised cruelty. I don't think *Mezza Voce* is a tender book. I think it is quite a violent book. That ís why I chose *Mezza Voce*, with half voice, that is, a counterpoint to the book's content. (*Long silence.*) I haven't reread *Mezza Voce* for a long time. I know there is a scene called "Theater." A completely Mallarméan passage.

JD: What is Mallarméan about it?

A-M A: What there is in all my writing and what strikes me is the descent of Igitur. Within limits, you must read *Mezza Voce* as a descent toward our ancestors to extinguish the candle.

JD: To blow out the candle.

A-M A: To blow out the candle. And Jouve, too, who marked me profoundly with his blasphemous side. I think that in *Mezza Voce* I have it too, there is this blasphemous side.

JD: You use theater to cover up, to erase speech, or rather there are two different parallel approaches, theater and speech...

A-M A: Two different approaches, theater and speech. I try to make them a single approach.

JD: When you write "in the reflection of speech several voices."

A-M A: It's still fiction. "In the reflection of speech several voices" is fiction. That is, there is a kind of multiplication of the one, of the he or the she who is silent and so a kind of chorus emerges.

JD: Choral element?

A-M A: Choral or ancient element.

JD: What do you mean by "ancestor?"

A-M A: "Ancestor" means root.

JD: Of what?

A-M A: It's the root of writing. It's the root of desire, of movement, of lyric, it is truly where I mine all possible forces. Once this descent is made, like a renascence, like a phoenix. (*Silence.*) A phoenix. And the more character increases and decreases, the more voice, song, graphic song seem important to me. I work them with white space. That is, the white space makes room for a decrease in voice. (*Silence.*) The suppression of theme is also this descent, suppression of a relationship to the real, of going beyond the real.

23

JD: Must there be knowledge in writing or in a written book?

A-M A: I don't think so.

JD: Or it is already too late.

A-M A: I don't know about "already too late." There is knowledge in immediate desire. Knowledge is not thought, considered, willed. It comes, it is beneath what is being written, but it does not arrive as support for what is being written, and even if I cite names...well known like Jouve, Bataille, Mallarmé, I do not write "after" their work but "after" the mark they have left in me.

JD: So *Mezza Voce* dates back to 1984.

A-M A: Yes.

JD: Now it is 1990.

A-M A: Yes.

JD: I can think of the formidable expanse of time...

A-M A: ...yes, yes...

JD: ...around you and ahead of you, that is basically a trove, a trove for reading, a trove of possibilities, or else...is it the opposite, something closing before you?

A-M A: It is something open. To the point where I refuse to know what I have written. I don't know anything by heart. I don't know. I don't even know what's in the books. (*Silence.*) I refuse to know. In fact, I hate knowledge. Passion is what I have for the authors cited.

JD: But what must no longer be known in order to attempt to stand naked before that opening, before writing's absence of desire? What is it you want to forget?

A-M A: I want to forget the oblivion remaining deep within me as trace, as scar, what I have written, as scar. I think there is a drive. I can speak of drive rather than knowledge. Drive and....

JD: But at what moment? At the moment of writing?

A-M A: At the moment of writing first it's the drive, then excessively reworking.

JD: ...yes....

A-M A: ...cold.

JD: I am thinking of the opening, the waiting. What do you place there, in that opening?

A-M A: The opening? There is a kind of antinomy between distance and opening. Distance leads one to believe that everything is far away and that the opening is a leap into the present. No — the opening is the implementation of lyric. Because I insist on keeping a cold lyricism, that is a lyricism...

JD: ...controlled?

A-M A: ...controlled, in quotes, in italics, with blanks. Thus it bypasses a certain rationality.

JD: It's what's in the book. I would like to go back to this waiting, from 1984...

A-M A: Ah!

JD: ...to 1990 where you appear to be doing nothing.

A-M A: No, I didn't appear to be doing anything.

JD: Would you talk to me about that semblance? What do you enter into that apparent not-working? I suppose there is no drive and there is no desire.

A-M A: Anxiety. In fact, in order to write I must have pleasure. And it happens that for years I did not experience enough pleasure to force me to write. Because even if what I write is hard or violent I think it always derives from pleasure and desire. And it happens that for years I haven't experienced any more of that pleasure. I am waiting for it. (*Laughs.*)

JD: Then how did the pleasure occur for writing *Travail vertical et blanc*?

A-M A: I work a lot on demand. And it happened that I was asked to write *Travail vertical et blanc*. I'll use the example of "Chemin de l'ermitage." I don't exactly know how, I found a photograph of a carnival in a small town and I began to experience great pleasure from this photograph and that pleasure permitted the text. (*Silence.*) But since then, I haven't found a single object of pleasure. So I think I can overcome the anxiety that keeps me from writing, but for the time being I haven't the means. I haven't found what stimulates me...

JD: ...what neutralizes the anxiety...

A-M A: ...what neutralizes the anxiety.

JD: That is, you let the anxiety...

A-M A: ...take over, yes. I have to, I have to feel completely free in order to write.

JD: It's a kind of protection...

A-M A: ...yes...

JD: ...the anxiety...

A-M A: ...no, really the anxiety is the stopping. The anxiety is unbearable. It is lived every day. It is lived every night. And, for the moment, not...

JD: No...

A-M A: Yes...

JD: As I know you, I can also imagine your playing with your anxiety.

A-M A: I play with anxiety, true, but not to the point of writing ...I don't get there. Yes. (*Silence.*)

JD: A form of work basically...

A-M A: Yes.

JD: Play.

A-M A: Yes. A kind of work. Now this makes several years of anxiety. (*Silence.*) But I play and it wins, it wins.

JD: Even so, throughout all the years of anxiety you have allowed yourself to attempt new themes. État, the score, *Mezza Voce*, the stage. What would be next? Tomorrow...

A-M A: Oh! Next, I think it would be...I am leaning toward a text more scattered on the page, more overtly lyrical. I saw it in *Travail vertical et blanc*. The more years that pass, the more writing seems to open up. Because État is very dense, very compact, *Mezza Voce* is already more open, in *Travail vertical et blanc*, there are blocks of prose. And in what I imagine being able to write, I imagine writing always using white space, blocks of prose. I am getting closer to a prose, to a writing that breathes differently.

JD: You are making a distinction between verse and a block of prose...

A-M A: No, not really, no. But I always need fiction. It is indispensable to me. I play, as you said. I play a game that perhaps will be articulated more violently. Even while seeming more gentle.

Because in *Travail vertical et blanc*, there is always the threat that I do not forget, "*you are there / dark*." And it really is a threat. And this threat has stalked me for years, since I am no longer able to write.

JD: Is it physical, this threat, or is it metaphysical?

A-M A: *(Laughs.)* It isn't physical. It isn't physical.

JD: Can you give an example of fiction, a model of fiction?

A-M A: A model of fiction. In *Anawratha*, there's a whole passage on the very brief encounter I had with someone who overwhelmed me with words I didn't understand and I made a whole text from it. That's a fiction. *(Noises.)* Do you find that the fiction in *Anawratha* is a good one?

JD: A barque is burning at the...?

A-M A: ...???...

JD: I really love that: "A barque is on fire at the embankment in the port."

A-M A: Oh yes! That is pain.

JD: "She was unaware that she would never again know that."

A-M A: Yes, that's literal. It seems to be a fiction but it's literal.

JD: Pain as fiction.

A-M A: Yes. It is literal. I really saw...a barque on fire at the embankment in the port and it is absolutely accurate, my existence was never the same afterwards. It is a cut in my life. But it is presented as pure fiction, while it is more than painful.

JD: So it would be in ...*Anawratha*...

A-M A: Yes...(*Reading from* Vocative Figure:) "The words he spoke mezza voce in a whirl of incestuous sheets he fled made her hear him as though paralyzed in an enchantment. From the gaze, above all from the gaze, from the mouth, and hands, the hair, above all the gaze, an imperfect labiality surrounded him, she the witness, flowers woven into necklaces of the night. His name is to be repeated; and an image, given to him, continued inside her. Their place?"...Wait, that's wrong! Oh yes, "Their tie fortuitous but swiftly shattered by the laws of chance."

*

Paris, December 8, 1990

A-M A: Well I just finished *Mezza Voce.*

JD: Yes. What did you think?

A-M A: ...

JD: What are your critical comments concerning *Mezza Voce*?

A-M A: My cri...

JD: Or, how was this rereading for you?

A-M A: I was astonished by what I could write. (*Laughter.*) And I asked myself, "Did I write this?"

JD: And what still astonishes you in this book?

A-M A: I noticed themes that keep reappearing.

JD: What?

A-M A: Song, hair, the body...

JD: What astonished me was the presence of memory.

A-M A: Memory, yes.

JD: Memory, the memorial thing, remembering, remembrance....
So I wonder if there isn't a kind of construction, a geometricizing starting from memory as though rigorously setting up a grid.

A-M A: Yes.

JD: On which you play out a game of terror.

A-M A: I do not play, but I speak of memory as part of the body because it is vastly a question of the body. It is very corporeal.

JD: The body is present.

A-M A: The body is very present. With wounds, ornaments, breath. Breath. Song that returns. There are, and this can be annoying, repeating themes, returning song, terror, terror in the tragic that I can call black, in the body *mis en abîme*. And there is a certain *jouissance* that allows the writing. (*Silence.*)

JD: Don't you think that verse only appears in a gap in the staging, in the absence of memory, or absence of...that it intervenes in moments of lack?

A-M A: Oh!

JD: How does it intervene? What are its means of appearing?

A-M A: The word?

JD: No, verse.

A-M A: Verse? Oh, verse! It's logic, it's structure. Without the whole works of parentheses, quotation marks, white space, verse ...shredded...I think it would only be a false...because the...

JD: What?

A-M A: Verse permits the breath, permits...verse permits...

JD: Suffocation as well...

A-M A: Yes.... No, no, I don't think so.

JD: There are, however, knots on the page. Knots of meaning, terrorized, knots of terror.

A-M A: Yes, but...

JD: Where the verse blends, contracts...

A-M A: Yes.

JD: No?

A-M A: Yes, but it's always ludic in some way. Even the terror is ludic. Yes.

JD: What other notes have you taken?

A-M A: I made them before reading *Mezza Voce*. (*She reads.*) "Biography tripled by fiction. Fiction and its ambiguous relationship with desire. Stripped bare in the abyss, desire springs forth anew in the lyric line. Ternary: double biography, desire and fiction. Consequence: addition of theater. Theater that multiplies or divides. Theater that divides, at once lyric, ornamental and cruel in the development of its discourse." There is also at times a certain cruelty. Existence of the terrible, there is the sense of the cruel. "One comes to the discursive which seems to dominate, a discursive sliced by space"....

JD: ...mmmm

A-M A: ..."a discursive sliced by space where breath appears." That's very important. Basically I can believe I am suffocating. But another breath comes...

JD: Yes.

31

A-M A: ...revives. Silence appears. So there is silence. "In this silence, instruction plays keeping up a parallel discourse, thus double, and which leaves room for the multiple while reuniting with the initial discourse. It's the negation of the fragment, supported by fragmentation." Yes, because what appear to be fragments are not. You know that. "Theatrical direction of body, wounds, and ornaments." And the bodies of others, I might add. "Ambiguous ornament, the corporeal in a temporality that plays on the body." That's all.

JD: One thing caught my attention: double biography.

A-M A: Yes.

JD: What's that.

A-M A: That's not at the first level. I don't want to reveal it. But I know what I'm referring to. I'm referring to my father. I'm referring to.... There are biographical references which are sublimated by fiction.

JD: By fiction?

A-M A: By fiction.

JD: By theatricality, you mean?

A-M A: Yes, by a fiction. By a fiction.

JD: Those notes were written before your reading?

A-M A: Before.

JD: And afterwards?

A-M A: I read this morning. And took no notes after.

JD: None....

A-M A: I only noticed that there are also repetitions in the text, too. Repetitions in the same text. And I noticed that song was very important. Song. In my life, too. That's why I can speak of biography...song had a great impact, too. I listened a lot to sopranos, countertenors.

JD: So, the voice.

A-M A: The voice.

JD: The theme of the voice is a permanent one.

A-M A: The voice is a permanent theme.

JD: Which reveals...

A-M A: ...lyric.

JD: I'll return to the question of verse. I wonder whether the poem doesn't adorn itself with verse in the light of sacrifice.

A-M A: There is sacrifice, yes.

JD: I wonder whether verse is not an element of blindness.

A-M A: I don't think so. I think it's the opposite. Verse is an element of light. And then verse brings the sacrifice theme into play, I mean the ...mystical aspect. There is a mystical aspect that is not obvious. But when I say in a text "I could not see him" I am thinking of Christ. I think of Christ.

JD: And what moves in the direction of sacrifice? The poem, the subject...the book moves toward sacrifice?

A-M A: No, no, no. It's not sacrifice. It is the sacrificial. There is no sacrifice. There is the sacrificial. And, basically, I make my body and the bodies of others sacrificial elements.

JD: I'll return to the question of verse. It seems to me that verse is a little like speech made up of non-speech, or of abstract speech.

A-M A: Yes, yes, yes. But sometimes verse provides all the lyricism. The white space provides the sacrificial.

JD: Why did you reread *Mezza Voce*, for example, and not *Figure vocative* or *Travail vertical et blanc*?

A-M A: Because *Travail vertical et blanc*, I'm afraid, I am afraid it will be my last book. That makes me afraid. But it interests me because the writing is somewhat different.

JD: A writing of opening.

A-M A: Yes. We were talking about that the other day.

JD: With jubilation and not with fear.

A-M A: No. But that book silences me, my books frighten me.

JD: Why? Are there shadows around them, in them?

A-M A: Well, here I return to the biographical, for the sake of the lived. That no one perceives. Only I can know. But the lived is truly sublimated. Because there is a text for Claude Royet-Journoud which comes out of an almost...mystical experience.

JD: Meaning?

A-M A: Meaning that...it is a little sensitive, I have to say.

JD: ...mmmm...

A-M A: I'll tell you.

JD: Yes.

A-M A: I was in the country and there were a lot of religious objects. There was a Christ with huge eyes. And I'm not sure how exactly, but I began to think I had been poisoned. I started to...I called a doctor. I started have trouble seeing, to have visual problems and I kept seeing the gaze of this Christ...and thought I was dying and my legs were stiff — my legs were stiff. The doctor said to me "Oh no!" and that woke me. Because my legs were stiff.

JD: A kind of numbness in the image of Christ.

A-M A: Yes

JD: ...

A-M A: No, no. Death, death.

JD: Beginning with an image.

A-M A: Beginning with an image.

JD: What did you make of it?

A-M A: Made nothing. Or nothing but a page that came out of a mystical or an hysterical experience.

JD: Beginning with an image.

A-M A: I really had the symptoms of someone who was going to die. That is...the tiles, I was seeing them double, and my legs got completely stiff. And afterwards, I wrote that text. But in fact I play, I play with...terror and I write only in its pleasure. (*Sigh.*)

JD: So what is there in that terror?

A-M A: And that terror, it often comes back in my text, terror. A very powerful word. It is made of attention...from a difficulty with attention, and then don't forget that there was a threat. There is a permanent threat all along...

JD: ...

A-M A: When I speak in another text of a "chain," it's a chain that isn't decoration, I am trying to give the body magical power. (*More quietly.*) Those ornaments are magic.

JD: And they protect from what?

A-M A: They are protection from terror. I must say that I am very attracted to equations, number, geometry, it seems to me that verse coheres there, the verse you spoke of. And then, with that geometry and those equations a counterpoint appears made in relation to a very painful lyricism that I can't deny.

JD: But who is asking you to deny it?

A-M A: No one! But Jean, if I don't have a geometrical, mathematical base, lyric would take the upper hand, and I don't want that. I deeply mistrust that. My initial outpouring is lyric. The sources I write from come out of desire. And there is always a kind of.... I am also talking about flagellation.

JD: ...

A-M A: I say pretty cruel words. There is, undeniably, a kind of cruelty in these texts. And also...geometry and numbers count for a lot in this cruelty.

JD: And how do you reconcile...flagellation and geometry? How do they come to punctuate the cruelty?

A-M A: Throughout the discourse. Throughout the discourse. Again, I noted themes which return incessantly throughout *Mezza Voce*: the body,...the breath, above all the body, the body, the body. A head of hair, a head of hair. I don't know whether to tell the story but my family was always...shamed by my hair.

JD: ...

A-M A: Very long and very thick hair, and my father refused to see me before he died because I went to see him at Curie with long hair. And there I take pleasure in speaking of a head of hair as ornament — but at the same time it's painful because I was rejected for this hair.

JD: And what exactly was forbidden?

The lack of distinction. Now I only wear a chignon. Because hair, for me, is sumptuous, and in spite of the condemnation of hair I love to put it into my texts.

JD: I'm going to show you the photographs. They are quite astonishing.

A-M A: Yes. The little girl? Yes, it's me. I was very young.

JD: And the German shepherd, your household pet.

A-M A: Yes, that was our dog...

JD: ...your pet.... And this one which I love so much.

A-M A: Oh yes! Me too.

JD: I've said to you that what you're combing there is already verse!

A-M A: Yes.

JD: With both hands.

A-M A: It was a lot of energy.

JD: In your wrists.

Joë Bousquet

from *Language Entire*

Suddenly I have to admit that language is not indiscriminately subjective or objective. The world, with all its events, erects
itself between the subjectivity and the objectivity of language.

A giant whose shadow is under the earth.

*

There are visions that seem to exclude you and that are,
meanwhile, full of your presence. There are visions that erase
you. There is your absence, and the vision that it is.

*

Paintings I have chosen presently cover the walls of the fitting
room which, since the tailor's death, I have made into my bedroom. They transformed the house, and I was at first not aware
of it, my imagination having been distracted by a more banal
fact: the fortunes of the move placed my bed in the same spot
where, long ago, I used to try on my suits. Leaning against the
partition from which the mirror had been taken down, from now
on I would languish in the place where for all those years I had
watched myself grow. This fact had blinded me. I attributed to it
the spell cast upon me so often by the sight of the paintings
gathered around my bed.

Langage entier, Rougerie, 1966

It was evening, I was looking at a painting by Fautrier, a chalky hedge bristling crystals of emerald green where flesh poked out, thick, compact like a breast but resisting any shred of resemblance. A living object at once like flesh and like mother-of-pearl but clenched like a fist upon its own form. The green could have been described as bristling with emerald lava under a blooming threatening nude increased by its depth like a hand ready to open.

But the most wonderful aspect of this painting was the ground from which the subject separated. The space around the object was not its shelter, but the reverse; thickened yet canceled by what was around it, not at ease but standing out, as though the thing and its surroundings were a contrast in depth. Fine trajectories like streams of ash burst out at several points from this suspended explosion, suggesting an attack on the atmosphere by their continuously shifting ways of clawing at it, of dismembering the cellular treasure of the depths where they had been illuminated. Finally, in this painting, something swelled before which extension did not shrink but sought to hold itself, and took on substance distancing itself, deceiving the eye with regard to its density, veiling the whole perspective.

Many words to provide the banal impression whose analogue is: in front of a threshing machine thickening the air radiating the heat of its inner workings while it seems to confuse the floor area where each person wends his way, bringing it work, fodder.

To one who looks at it with no assumptions, Fautrier's painting very simply reveals the source of space in an object.

I looked around at all the paintings covering the walls, some here, some there: ones that, revolutionary or not, accept the given that space is equal to itself, that it shelters itself and that objects inhabit it like a rock the sea. But abruptly, with Fautrier, already, with Max Ernst, a first unforgettable fact: the object is not in the space, it is the source of it, the contained source. One could say it engenders it while resisting it.

Like hazy nausea the memory of the tiny metal clock hideously named alarm comes back to me. Its ticking denied space, its ticking measured out an abstract space with no link to the present. I could not hear it then without eliminating myself from extension, without discovering a beyond which I entered like a mirror's reflection. (The world where space contains objects is conceivable and we can enter it, it is the real outside of being, this life in the state of fiction where painting explodes the major phenomenon of life like unforgettable evidence: space is progeny of the object.)

The object contains the roots of space. The object translated into effigy has come with its roots, and these roots were well-springs.

This destruction of time where space is swallowed up is unbearable. One is dying to breathe in the street where gaze and gesture beat time and space together, where having become objects and the wellspring of extension again, one escapes the fiction of an immaterial time which (produces space without meeting bodies).

(The worst pain is that he no longer feels the distress. His sadness is to live without being able to suffer it.)

A painter has used a canvas to fish for an object: he has seen that extension was the blood of things and the radiance of our own blood.

*

The disappeared share our life without ever revealing themselves. Their existence does not separate them from what we are. But what we believe we are excludes them.

Danielle Collobert

Survival

I leaving voice without response to articulate sometimes words
that silence response to other ear never
if to muteness world not a sound
plunges into blue cosmos
no more question that vertical journey
I leaving slide to horizon
all equal all mortal leaving starting with the I
at full speed fleeing the horizon
at last to hear only music in the screams
enough enough
exit
entering born on garbage hardly recognized ground
emerged from salty slime the fetus come out of the drain
solar plexus eaten away anguish diffusing lungs breath gasping

*

squeezed the neck by the cord waking
shivering waking
burned consumed *bonze*
body break
outside of hands caresses
far from lips drank
memory of the body
letting go present moment survival
not knowing on what to open energy to imaginary answered

Survie, Orange Export, 1978

stuttering hardly at the rips
the screams from the edges of wounds no enough
dove black into the bloodbath
to work the veins for words
I speech opening mouth open to say I live to whom
swung weaponless to chaos
will survive or not resistance to blows all life long
I gone the exploration of the void
groping against day
already manacles on the hands brands on the wrists

*

at the feet irons chains
the distance of a step the unit of measure
I scraping my earth with that
drag the noise through space
first of all on the tape sound of Prometheus
vulture in throat
at blows to blood beaten back endlessly toward silence
in the middle of the forehead the flat future desert
behind hidden perhaps the body to be pulled together

*

little living cell with searching head
going wanting desperately to stick its juice somewhere
goodness at mucosa the waiting at orifices
the silent first celebration of life
swallowed up by lava flow sticking speech wall between which
nothing to do to get the sounds out beyond barely death
stretching nerves to tune up the sound the lips higher
the bone skull resounded
strangulation overtone to hold barely beyond death
or not smiling an empty smile in dark reflections face extinguished
hardly light from distant sight
pour the seven days of circular hell

creation torments and rest included
sleep full of earth and dreams included

*

whose the sun sometimes music on wide sky of open
flat on back the separated
the sheltered likely freely drawing on the thrust of the bearable
from over there from pretty deep the written on body
I etching in grit the erased moment
to push fever to the reverberating lips the gong
or buzzing rhomb fleeing the head
or drums of survival
or dry desert dust bombs
and still flames licking the body of fear
I of living insect nailed to the wall
seeking living to suffering more
dreaming it nightly even
in view of the definitive

*

I time of what
spreading
wave rolled to gaze
untiringly from the I liquid measured red
fragments imperceptible to little eye of time vision none
onto space never more than a broad field
the rest open to the rower celestial visions
to suck from sentences toothless sustenance
I crushing sounds syllables magma telluric jolts
or won be the tidal wave footing lost in the basement syntax
days of passion
light from veins which comes
into surface articulation
I say blazing energy the scream or like burns never said

Edith Dahan

Giudecca

20th Century: literature

great axes that bind the whole north-Asiatic continent, from European Russia to the Japan Sea, literature, the great edifices, stations, domes, glass structures, vaulted arches, power stations, railroads. I go back up the boulevard Sebastopol as far as the Gare de l'Est, archives and museums, frescos of ground pigment, entry to the major lines: Munich Berlin Schedule.

Rereadings, mountain meadows, I see mountain masses unrolling, rivers, forests. Collages and ancient works, Sigismund, years of maturity followed by years of an intense suffering in London. At the corner of the boulevard Sebastopol I pick up again, streets, passages, processions of Haussman facades going towards the river.

*

The war had arisen abruptly once the major lines of the European network had connected with the Asian border.

I am writing words, the last words of the day, at times this gentle shift of light, in the window's gap opening onto the Venetian docks, in the breadth of the window's opening onto the Armory, quays, warehouses, factories, corridors, palaces, the taut awning over the Atlantic wall of the San Michele cemetery.

---

fig., No. 1 (1989)

The first main period begins the day before the war. In *The Black Circle* of beings and things, a painter sees the world as a succession of tonalities and internal resonances, an incandescence of sounds and of sense. It snowed in me and I awoke, breast afire before wheat fields, and the world again present, in clouds that pass, illness-birth, illness-birth, rereading all of Tolstoy, illness-birth, rereading all the Russians, cycles of the years 1905-1919, and I awoke, the window open, before the great unfurling of clouds, the world which was passing, undertow, East wind, Firebird in the river's prosody.

*

Since this morning, above the ocean the rhythm of books, the beat of sentences, breath of each word, full ocean color, aerial blue above the sea, opening of the field, transparency of light when the season's motion decenters filling the sky, vision of the open city, motion of sentences, the year revolves around Mars. Gentle shift of light, other rhythms appear, diffuse seasons of fabrics, morning burst of crossing to retrieve the words and the voice in the bright night ocean, each one of the words. Closest to their internal power, retrieving that particular tonality of the word blue, coolness of the morning on the Brenta.

*

Slow spaces of water, studios, hangars, the filmed city's level approach, holds, basins, wide angle, industrial smoke, foundries, basins, watery blue film stock in the opening of the field, wharves, domes, processions of holds and warehouses, discolored areas of the river, towards the most isolated regions on the coast, chimneys, mist, pylons of reinforced concrete, vacant lots blending with currents of sand, boats filled with water going upstream towards Giudecca, long shot on the rare walkers, travelers, Titian, Philip of Commynes, quays, stockades, fortifications controlling the great axes of navigation to the East, the commercial routes to the North, forests of the Alps, Balkans, thousands of trees, entire forests, boles of oak and elm under the cobbles of the city giving onto the sea.

*

Nakedness of the sky, skin's coldness to the touch, at the crossroads of the lines of the past, archives and museums, mountain meadows.

Young woman withdrawing, the novel's central episode. The first sketches date to 1909. She was reading, an ancient interior sea left traces of fire.

*

On the right the mountains and further off the sea.

This morning I awoke in the middle of you, in the middle of parks, in the middle of words, long walks, corridors and quays, the Salute's pavement. Motion of waves, great tide cycles. Snow covers the city and several times the word torment. That year, 1909. Schoenberg wrote the *Three Pieces for Piano*. They were completed in Berlin in 1911, Cézanne's last canvases. How to write to you these last few months, this work on the motif, extension and regrouping of themes around Prague Vienna Budapest. The city is silent and I am at my table listening to the ebb and flow of the waves, the pressure on the words opening the way — first piece of Opus II, completed in 1909.

*

I am listening to a child all existence is burning.

Through the foliage and nocturnal dynasties, sexually the woman swimmer enveloped by the waves follows after this circular door opening into the waves and the oceans. Moved along by the currents, a woman swims back up myths and forests, beyond sleep, enormous vessels and distant shores, sailings, childhoods, golds and meadows of Ravenna, a nativity, lying in the flow of the river, glimmers of legends, lyric time, second suite of time, motions of vessels, foliage and gods at the water's surface.

*

In the river's slowness, in the slowness of the sentences, run-off of overcast walls and grounds, palaces and orchards, multi-colored facades, in the slowness of the divinities and of rivers, vines and meadows settled by sleep, words' bewildered power, sentences all in curves, sexually the woman, ellipses and rhythms at shoulder level, in circles' arcs, all in sunlight, swims against the current of strange fears, of dark noises at the water's surface, in turn such stretch of words, of sentences abandoned to time.

*

Seated beside the light, Tyrrhenian, a shadow carried by the wind system, in the night and the fury, the sea crossed the trees and the lands, glimmer of the legends. Black arc of the Appenines, islands, Mediterranean forests. I am the child who sees through the blinding wellspring of sleep, temple against the garden's iron balustrade, phosphorous blues bordering the forest. I hear the dark murmurs of the vessels, the current of sentences in the distance on the page. We are measure of god, offerings, rhythms and riverbanks of time. Adrien goes down under the snow, slow motion, the sky coils around the word red.

*

Today I am not writing, I am seeing to the house of writing, and you are there, in the garden light.

47

André du Bouchet

from *Journals 1952-1956*

September 1954

With a few
    years'
        delay
I have restored it all

I have found you again

with no mouth and no voice

in a house whose walls
have been completely removed
            and which has been returned to me

air

            this white nest

                    *

Carnets 1952-1956, Plon, 1990

Poetry is nothing but a certain astonishment before the world and the means for this astonishment.

November 1954

I only can keep you
      by what separates us

*

when the wall, cleared
vanishes
true painting
but followed as far as its destruction, the poem also is a painting

...I would like to save
                    air
but everything is ruthlessly brought back to the line.

*

What Cézanne felt so deeply: those separate trees, so distinctly separated one from the other —, that join at the top

*

...one only sees by means of this separation — and it is also by means of this separation that one stops seeing.

This love of the impossible creates another object — possible,
but different,
                              — poetry.

December 1954

I have learned to suppress. Suppress — rather than omit

...And before the inexhaustible world, what remains of the
being without breath
          like a branch in the dry air.

February 1955

                                        being devoured
          by what separates me
                                        from you

     I will be no more than thickness

                    blank extension

                              *

...I have cut out what could appear to be a sigh, to stop myself
on the brink of the line of light.

                              ...stopping before the image
is out of breath — and subtracting to only the traces.

March 1955

Necessity appears in Art when it is no longer necessary that this be before or after — in front or behind — when the plausible sequences are reversible.

*

We are not of this world. We are from the future world. But the rest is dead.

We are present, but not here.

And yet, place is everything.

*

Double polarization of images. "The rosy-fingered dawn." At the same time what can touch and what, without reaching it, you see.

Who can say whether in the crystallizing of an image such as *Pools of Glass* it's the shattering or the freezing — what changes its form — that carries it.
There is a law of the polarization of images, set against their opposite.
The image inhabits its past and its future.

*

Exhaustion of seeing, and what I feel at moments ripening there, plunges me into speechlessness.

May 1955

I would like to prolong the moment
when man flies

                                and my joy
in that explosion

...the white evening

          like a great
                angle

...emptiness breathes me, yanks me
out of my rut.

                    *

I admit the
wound and the
fire — and
this earth
also, marvelously —
                    wound and distance
I so feel her, — far from earth, — the one who meets me.

                    *

Our wildness blends with the light

The weight of simple things is so difficult to bear.

June 1955

The clumsiness of almost all the commentaries.

Yet we find ourselves in front of this: a verbal infinite, which affords us access to something that remains to be said —, although there is no obligation to say it.

*

Poetic perception, as opposed to critical perception, is seeing the separation, the distinction —, rather than what is separate.

Hölderlin sees that it has to do with an image — with a reflection, not the thing — but the image in its turn becomes so simple that he can not speak of it.

So it has to do with a perception that leads to silence rather than to exegesis.

*

> You will be the poem
> thirsty for air
> that suffocates in
> > the air

*

"I was dead...and I was still waiting" (Baudelaire)

This "death," always expected elsewhere, arrives here unexpectedly, but contradicting "representation;" it seems nonetheless, to a certain degree, tied to it.

...There is simultaneity of experience and of representation—
if the logical order does not appear to have purchase on experience,
there is concomitance between the formula and what escapes it.

July 1955

This death is always imagined — and this imagining is always
infallible since it models itself on what is known

— infallible and infertile imagination.

...this death become memory does not suppress the real
death, on which poetry has no purchase.

— this displacement between mortal poetry — death in
poetry — and death without poetry.

...Poetry is invested in a link to this will — this appetite —
only moves on by making the object withdraw that it seeks to
ascribe.

In this absence Baudelaire finds his singularity.

Death is what he cannot imagine — but it is by means of this
very impossibility to imagine — this emptiness — that he reveals
his presence.

At his moment of waking, Baudelaire knows his death. This
emptiness is an opening.

*

...awakening, I knew my
death — eternity of dust

*

I drink dusk like a gulp of wine

*

                    ...I stretch into the transparency
of my disappearance.

*

    poem
            leaving
    on this fault

    like a light illuminated
    at the ends of
    the earth

*

    alone
            what is extreme
    is entitled to air

*

                                        ...the altitude
of poetry above regular life.
    But I don't lose sight of what annihilates me.

                              *

    It isn't a particular memory that moves me.
    It isn't those feet in the snow, but something that has not yet
arrived and which pushes us on.

                              *

    Baudelaire seeks the singularly different, the Invariable: that
which stays the same, and which he can only conceive as
particularly different from what he is.

    ...he wants to draw the same into the other.

    It is that familiar, that already seen, which is something other
than what he wanted to do.

    What he wanted to grasp is the other — the new unknown —
and take from it what is infallible in it. To take what awaits him
at face value.

    Different is same. But same is also different.

...Wait of the poem —
never denied —

                    even by
the poem

    ...From the poem he experienced only this emptiness — the
transparency of the "terrible dawn" — this common bond of

death and life where one appears through the other — just that.

Les Phares: what shines is the appeal.

B. who stretches into the sky of divergence.

August 1955

here the day agrees
                            with my step
I slip at once on the snow
of paper and on this dry
earth

*

                                        ...earth runs for a moment
in several opposing directions — I am stunned
by this clash.

*

...Air fresh to the open mouth. Air
that does not stop.
                            But I would have been this
lacuna.

*

I only have on me this letter to which I am attached and which no longer has a name — only the sky is left to separate the lines.

*

I will repeat myself like earth you tread. I will reveal my monotony.

*

...poet, stopped before the same grass —, my burnt feet.

Baudelaire always projects the already done. Poetry is the unknown that intervenes, that is determined by the realization of the project, the grain of sand that alters the repetition — that makes it diverge.

Thus his poetry is even guilty — identifies with defeat — with the absence nothing could fill, with the unforeseen.

Baudelaire is grandiose — he is never what he projects himself to be — and he is forced to believe in a project — his project is to be infallible.

What is infallible is his defeat.

Paule: *I'm so hot I want to take my skin off—, and the sun to go away.*

*

In the poem revealed —

this transparency

58

I have revealed only my
sickness — I cannot dwell
on this sickness

— transparent

...I brought back
the day

to earth

and from this day
I made my earth

October 1955

The "particular evil" of the poem (Baudelaire)

...this wait that arouses it and that follows it.

Poetry is this nothing —, but a nothing that cancels the rest.

*

...and yet I expected
so much
from arid
day

...Something old

...The glow was always there — weakly it lifted me. I waited for
the flames.

And I was still waiting.

    ...frozen
             wait
    I have known your
               shoulders

    of me or of the day
    which will last

        *

    I would have liked
        to move the earth

        *

    to be
             is enough
    keeps fire's
         place

The being — outside — has no woman's or man's name.

        *

If one can venture to speak of the poem's being, it is precisely that the knot of being forms itself exactly in its expression.

        *

...promise, I kept you
like blank paper

that great trove of earth
         and sky

           I move into

                    *

September 1956

Shakespeare's rhythm is the fundamental principle of his
poetry. It is the motivating force that determines the rapid alternation of question and answer —, that rules the duration of the
periods.

This rhythm is the product of an unequalled brevity permit-
ting inclusion, in a single iamb, of an aphorism composed of two
contradictory propositions —, and then some.

It is the rhythm of the free individual who refuses idols and
thus is able to be sincere, laconic.

                    *

(about Joyce's last book)

In its measure —, can't be translated.

— where, being, it is without that opening, that reflected
imprecision — by which a poem communicates and radiates.

Work which *being* — does not *come across.*

...So here is the *unthinkable* work which, if worst came to worst, would go unread, but which meanwhile *is*.

It is in that available field of the poem which authorizes each reader to make what he encounters his own, and forget what remains irreducible to him — that at the same time the possibility of its translation creeps in.

In the *written* world, reduced to the letter — there must meanwhile exist — even in J. —, an indeterminate place, an unwritten place — that holds itself back — and opens the book — incites reading.

This unknown — this hiatus, that is the end of the book...

Dominique Fourcade

The Sentence

The sentence always translated from an other language, the
sentence unfounded, the sentence of liquid shadows beyond
which we do not look, writing it,

zuk, No. 24 (Sept. 1989)

Liliane Giraudon

Jean Daive: Neutral in a Still Room

Jean Daive:	
Décimale blanche	Mercure de France, 1976, 80 pp.
Fut bâti	Gallimard, 1973, 112 pp.
Le jeu des séries scéniques	Flammarion, 1976, 96 pp., Coll. "Textes"
1,2 de la série non aperçue	Flammarion, 1976, 160 pp,. Coll. "Textes"
n, m, u	Orange Export, 1977, 24 pp.
Sllt	Givre, 1977.

> *Each act refers itself to paper, for contemplation*
> *without a trace becomes evanescent.*
> S. Mallarmé

The impossibility of saying, an "incisive mutilation of the body," moves through writing. A share of contemporary poetry stirs within this contradiction.

His back as though leaning on the color of the corners, Jean Daive pursues work which, since the 60's, and along with that of poets like André Breton or Roger Giroux, brings to light a new attempt at configuring verse.

In this place, verse (where the verb flashes in ignorance of its complement) would test

"silence single luxury after rhyme."

Critique, No. 385/6 (Juin-Juillet 1979)

It is under this rubric that Jacques Roubaud, in *La Vieillesse d'Alexandre*,[1] tries to situate a *practice* where "the verse unit, at the edge of division made obvious, is the unit, inhabits that fraction of the totality of space made visible.... Then moves, stops being anchored at the left of the line. As verse stops immediately following verse, detaches itself from it near the bottom, near the top, it also begins to move towards the interior of the lines in the rectangular paper space, in mind still squared off...

Since *Décimale blanche*, whose first line repeats the title, thus restoring a faultless nakedness and already inscribing it into a double neutrality

white decimal

on the edge of space

in order, crossing the opacity of the page, bordered and flat, to come to initiate there a singular project, that of blending a "wanting to be silent"[2] with the strength of a *récit* in where

a little of rat a little of dad

would not cease to be swallowed up, while

speech that placed death into my mouth

still breathed, every *given* uniting with a dead weight's own violence that would establish a deviation between grammar and body.

In the weft of support it is a mutilation that the *énoncé* supports and denounces:

who goes to the most high, from the negation of the work, goes from castration to something of death: page after page, corpse after corpse. A liturgy.

---

1. *La vieillesse d'Alexandre*, Maspero Ed., Coll. "Action-Poétique," 1989
2. Cf. Pascal Quignard.

The *énoncé* subtracts a body that distorts its own grammar with the pursuit always — sometimes empty, sometimes contained — of a fiction of characters like colors.

Body and cipher, it is sleight of hand like death.

The very body of the offense becomes the verse. Shattering its *élan* by successive rejections, it *details* a caesura: thus presenting it better. Astonishing posture, the one who speaks takes responsibility for the feminine of the trace like that of the cipher.

> *I am the nakedness*
> *of a brother and of a sister*

while

> *between earth and sky*
> *floats a grave the size*
> *of a meal*

An inversion threatens identity while the very landscape, *outside*, surrenders copy from an exchange where it is really the light that shadow threatens.

The body, like the letter, is divided: "n, m, u" reverse in pieces of downstrokes to reduce the elaboration of this: "It: cadastre of m."

A veritable organization of *dismemberment* mutilates the body, the *page* having in reality to do with the *skin* just as the letter can have its carnal application.

As Anne-Marie Albiach[3] writes, it has to do with a "cruelty of language in relation to the image of the letter and to the corporeal image."

If the cipher too alternates with the letter it is that all continuity reverses or, rather, *bites its tail*, thus: "1 7 10 16," whose cover is also the first page of the book (no more inside or outside of

---

3. "La déperdition de chance" (on Claude Royet-Journoud's *Le drap maternel ou la restitution*, Orange Export Ltd., 1977) in *Digraphe*, No. 16 (October 1978).

paper) becomes : "16 10 7 1," and the operation of reversal mimes the violence of writing

black   black and white.

Since always "speaking burns" and "the trace begins when fiction articulates the contours of a reading," the page becomes the place of a mutilation that language recovers and articulates. The very remarkable little collection *Sllt* bears witness to this: there again a speech establishes itself without reparable extension, struck by the neutral in a still room.

I must sit down
is
the world constitutes nothing, a disappearance
missing facing. On the right
is the parsley.
To the left the stroke I come from.

Sllt will prolong itself elsewhere in fragments[4] where it will be said:

But it is also true that we have not yet
spoken.

However:

The quantity of water or the mutation
announce the mirror
you carry. We are leaving the field.

A departure where the voice would pursue, in the attraction of language, a syllabic body that would not stop covering up the obscene nakedness of its limbs...

---

4. Cf. *Action poétique*, No. 77: "Comment nous écrivons" (April 1979).

Liliane Giraudon / Joseph Guglielmi

*4 Questions for Liliane Giraudon
from Joseph Guglielmi Concerning Giraudon's*
Divagation des chiens (P.O.L 1988)

Joseph Guglielmi: Why, in the book, this co-habitation, this prose-poetry montage?

Liliane Giraudon: What amazes me is that this question comes up every time. First, with *Je marche ou je m'endors,* then with *La réserve* and now with *Divagation des chiens.* The truth is that in all three of these books the mix of prose-poetry never is not present, and that it repeats itself in an almost programmatic way. In the beginning I didn't know why. But it seemed evident to me that the alternating "pieces from the notebook" (prose) should not be separated from the poems. From the poem, I should say. Because, in time, I saw that this little dark working into language pursued itself like an incessant murmuring inseparable from *amor fati,* from love of fate. Of course, I am referring to the fate of language. This maternal thing in which I bathe, move around, and often suffocate.

This summer, on a riverbank, someone explained to me the appearance of *prosimetron,* the mixing of prose and verse in the Gathas of the *Avesta* and in the Latin "Satura," trying to point out to me the non-aleatory nature of my predilection for this kind of *Mélange.* That really made me laugh. But, to get on with it, and to return to the term "pieces" (from the notebook) that

Banana Split, No. 23-24 (1988)

indicate theprose sequences, I must have felt that some people experience prose as a cheaper cut, in opposition to the poem object, or "verse" standard. But, no, I don't buy that. For me, the stakes are the same. Arising from the same rage, the same desire. The alternating verse-prose says what it says "in saying it." It participates in a poetic form.

"In poetry, you must locate yourself in poetry." It was not I who said that. I move ahead in the sand, often without even being able to speak in my own name.

JG: But this *mélange*, is it to challenge poetry, or the opposite, to increase the breadth of the poem, thereby maintaining an integrity of the self?

LG: There is, without doubt, something close to what has been called poetry-hate [*La haine de la poésie*]. Disappointment, too. But, finally, all that tied to a history of survival. Perhaps. I read, a few days ago, a dialogue between a journalist and an Indian. To the "white" formulation, "you are an Indian," the Indian replied, "I was an Indian." And it was at the same time an assertion and redress.

There is something on that order today in the fact of persisting in writing poetry.... Which has nothing to do with the little corporationist stakes deployed here and there. To persist, in this love/abhorrence of language, to persevere in a singularity of speaking. A necessarily minority speaking, nicely separate. But which attempts something within itself. As for what you call the integrity of the self, I don't know. It seems to me that this story of the self appears everywhere else. No more here than elsewhere. In *Divagation des chiens*, there are characters, situations, locations (cities, landscapes), and someone moving and looking who records it or can't. Doesn't have the strength. But that subject would be, how to say, intransitive. And then "she" isn't "me," and the story, if there is one, is without action. For daily use, almost domestic.

JG: This articulation goes as far as to use correspondence, why?

LG: There too, that's just submission to a genre. The more lost I am, the less I know where I shift and the more I impose constraints. Everlasting old-fashioned formal things from an epistolary novel that I used in *La Nuit* and then, closer to us, the introduction of letters, like in Zukovsky [sic] for example. I think of him because I recently learned fascinating things about the stages of construction of *A*, his lifelong poem, and about his relationship to correspondence.

I have always wanted to integrate letters into the poem. Real or false. At thirteen, my first long poem, a failure, almost immediately destroyed, incorporated a correspondence between a dead man and his daughter into the *alexandrines* (I had a terrible time with the silent e's, I could never "extinguish" them). The dead man wrote. Finally revealing a secret. The poem quoted 3 letters that didn't arrive. It was terrifying. But the worst, and I remember it very well, was the idea of setting this prose into the interior of the poem. Integrating the text of the letter. I made a nun who also taught me Latin read part of what I had written, and I remember her horrified by my audacity, telling me, "You cannot..." I had opposed a categorical refusal to her proposition to put the correspondence in verse.... Today I still have the memory of something extremely violent. She said something along the lines of "well, daughter, you must give it up, you will never be a poet...." I immediately turned my interest to horses, and, for a time, this passion replaced poetry.... But I wrecked my knee, not my hand.... But that is neither here nor there. But after all, underneath it all, it was without doubt fundamental. Increasingly, correspondence is for me something inseparable from the necessity of reading-writing. In *Divagation des chiens*, the epistolary fragments function as anonymous fictional sequences that repitch the question: why poetry?... That the letters have been received or not is not significant in itself, even if the epistolary game situates as central for me. To write or receive a letter is a daily concern. To the point that, at this moment, with the postal strike (and in Marseilles, it is especially effective), I am completely disoriented. What good is writing letters that won't arrive? I have a pile of them in a drawer. I paint on the envelopes. When the mail service resumes, they won't have the same meaning....

JG: But this book, is it not, all things considered, a book of morals not mortality?

LG: I don't know. Maybe. Because you can just as easily reverse it. That is, begin at the end and finish with the beginning. But *Divagation des chiens* is also, years later, a sort of attempt to respond (privately, very privately) to a book which, at that time, seemed to me to make a hole in the poetic discourse. It was *Louve basse* by Denis Roche. That's where the dog's furious face comes from. And the traitor's. I picked it up again a few days ago, and I discovered something that had completely escaped me: initially his project was to have been called *La femme et la prose*....

Joseph Guglielmi

The But Too White: fables

for Raoul

but the tablet where he will have le
veled merged with the air, silence such
white speech the voice: where the volume o
f that speech and what is outside
language; the but hole in the lan
guage what lights the bottom of the cav
ern. Watching the shky rip rip
ple so the change of the ch
ange destroyed by by the words
nary whose voice is mi
ne

*

dition and across the voice the thr
oat
white
cables   in Marshan
in the daye ylike   curri
cue cum you *but a shadow bea*
ring a man of their volup
tuous congress, *the chance, white in the*
day...white...Somna ..

Le mais trop blanc: Fables, Orange Export, Inc., 1977

72

*

"but dictated by the *desire* to brea
K with my solitude," *sucha a v*
oice for me, my hands (are) red, whi
te, Louis, these delicious mouth
fuls; from the palace like a glove
facing this leaf but too white:::
mojo working, move the lines but this s
un, but too blue: those who a
re good at preparing the bodies, b
read, stews, the vine, a sp
eech articulated like oil l
ike woords from the rising t
ake the dark street n a roo
m in *Quayaquil* n his drie
d up ha nd swimming despera-

*

spirit cool and distant, questions
about al*cool* in order to run a
ground on board a crippled ship,
candida — *Redde codicillos pos*
sunt occidere et redire soles — Ten'
provincia narrat bellam esse. Tube.
Supinus, appeared hair in the
reverse of air on his face, his
neither Whiteness nor Reflection, nor dreaming
of our escaping where the volume d

*

Whitened cold at the mouth. grows
bigger and bigger so flat at white
end so sleek White Paper; exam
Ple if my name was these scraps this
size that of their skin of the whise s
weat is ink. Head stu
ck n tightened the yellow-ass-sex.
number of our drilling laying yes
our luvs, wrote with his lim
pids and excellents flautists of hi
S left index.

*

                                   Clic hs unit let
sread *wonderful scraps* (repeat) to the
hospital and this bridge over the river "
la coppia giovane, soli, capelli S
elvaggi..ti dilata, ti conforta l'
intimo..." Simpatia della cose lon
tane, e non ci sono più parole: "n.
n": bet what lights whites n
the ink white day for me my h
and in the stream of alcohol questo lav
oro di ripulitura e di polizia, e
di teorie nuove di mondiali::: my
memories of   if the will t
o silence to palliate the divine ab
sence of speech vine of speech to ad
ress to that people; deprived of image

*

s movements evoking light th
is evening in characters of night the rea
ding with rage at Piombino, unloa
ding his load of light live.
Lighting frozen: "when were that white
screams rising..."   Cave
Yard of Age: air like a wa
ter sweet dairy, soft voice n the
grass on me rollin their
delicate bodies. Meaning was eaten,
Total dissatisfaction. The blood was
refreshed; on the white face, powdered
traces of death (   )

*

opening *The White Metro:* p. 16: "*Smoke
from dead cigarette — Encre de Chine shirt
floating...* it was written — opened veins
near a pond... — some guy agonizing
The speakeasy etc...etc.*" A silvered sky, cig
arette butts thrown on the ground, torn aqua
tints, a white hand to grab him slips on
theys bed of night with *addio del vecchio sol
e,* another blue hand who does u.
The whole burning sky galaxies chosen the
place to sleep... Choosing his body empt
of a guy is cool, shit-birds, caresses the cold fl
esh across the slant of

*

bone or the light of an end of after
Noon. the black and white snow, plots
grandeur, strength and rhythm (port
rait by V. Bell) smile, hollow, blue
window of white sun, hollow smiles:
the waters pile up their rockery... W
ite spit there are numerous leaves
exploded number
of our drillings. Clic. Clic. Clic. So pa
per white, white: "The damp slit of
a mother" Whats lucky page capta ac des
erta aversa velleribus niueis. Seeing 2
suns, more ferae: the breath resemb
led the breath of the

*

asphyxia, solitude of the book's head and
alone at every crisis a detail is c ut isol
ated convention. Sheet of white water of trans
mitted meaning, a slice into sense, n as i
f *empty of sense* in adornable white, opa
city of a barbarian hand wear away the br
eadth blue upon white, the opening onto bro
ke, speeches forblank themselves words

Joseph Guglielmi

The Radical Cut

"this cooing low and cut"... As the title and the first words indicate, Michel Couturier's *L'Ablatif absolu* places itself under the sign of the cut, of the separation, in this tearing where, infinitely, the "I" takes a schizo form...

In *cut sections*, like a fragmented moving picture, are imposed fragments, facets of a composition all starts where the *articulation of desire* posits the loss of the writing subject, its objective blinding, its *abstraction:*

> in the movement the aureole in deposits
> leaving marks shadows
> stains...

It is a meditation on the propagation of light, on variations of form and their deformations, on the relation of colors, their exact modulations in space, their erasure in *the uncoupled order*... gaping between the *walls* reproducing a world without reassuring images...

Where the gaze cuts matter, death emerges, extreme transparency, punctuation in blanks and folds, mutation of the *breath* memorized by the visible cut, *ablation* inscribed in the page *without theme. The word stretched* (to breaking) on the impenetrable *screen*, meets caesuras, the *word* exported by the *course* of the *exact* pagination delivers not its knot of enigma but opens there...

Le Dégagement multiple, Le Collet de Buffle, 1976

Division is the only connection, the single rule. In this cutting order, injunction reiterates until it provokes a *suspense of intervals,* a multidimensional *dissipating* system: mobility in the *open* of a *game* which requires an asyntagmatic deciphering. The meaning of *rapid montages* of discourse constantly reverse, unhook, and send us back into *a pre-place* where the image distorts. The text designates, meanwhile, always and forcefully, its disjointed movements, its abrupt turns, its overall curve of tension. Thus *an admirable mastery* of the gesture of writing and *reading* is released from the work of Michel Couturier. His book, in spite of the suspensions and starts, presents a condensed and obvious fabric. Plain of turbulence where the textual surface, in the vacillation of signifiers, does not compromise at any moment the infrangible unity of the proceeding. Nor the coherence (co-errance) of the architecture:

> a consonant
> would be there to hear to place
> in the fabric this unity
> of shadow
> ...
> to the white that holds
> the ease and drift of blue...

...in moving succession, a *eurythmic* orientation is orchestrated. The adjustment of the partition / composition (color or music) reveals an invariance whose *multiple function* does not cut into the play or the practice.

In *the open chain* of *L'Ablatif absolu,* Palanzuelo etches five moments of punctuation based on the sections of the book: *l'ablatif absolu, prologue, propos, occupation, épilogue.*

Palanzuelo's etchings are a reading that is all *cut sections:* a cut at several levels, first shattering color at the periphery, suspending it in precise islands carved against the emptiness where light ships out. Then, taking it up again in a three-dimensional space where the severed planes join and suggest... Exteriorities placed at distances where color, seized in their intersections, provokes the sign; mountain or flower (?) whose *subtle* stripping brightens.

The gaze, from the *abstract entity* of the poem to the demand of volume, tests the *major inoccupation*: the two *subjects* in pure loss.

In *Constante parité*, Michel Couturier pushes further, perhaps, the cesuraed stride of *L'Ablatif absolu*. The *fractioning* in the work achieves the *full gap*. There, by the interrogation of the *whole fraction*, one is at the extreme opening of discourse *without model*, neutralized by numeration, scanned by *setting to number*.

As if suspicion of the letter in its regulated sense wanted, through innovative tension, to precipitate the *course* of the shattering and the flagrant diversion of the *forbidden*.

Joseph Guglielmi

Abiography

> Biography, title first chosen then rejected
> with spirit, but recovered with a new
> meaning, full and even redundant, since
> life could never be separated from writing.
>
> (Roger Laporte)

how read it
   line after line
      given
     one look
    refresh the eyes
  against the abyss
      (Larry Eigner)

How to read Roger Laporte's book *Fugue*? And why borrow this question from Larry Eigner, if not to suggest that here, as there, a game is in play which reduces the page to "ruined archival theater".... Here and there "another time" (keeping in mind that *another time in fragments* is the title of a Larry Eigner book) invents itself whose *fragmentary power* reaffirms the inextinguishable creativity of human language, the inexhaustible "fountain of youth," the forever-knotted Reverdian *"thread of ink"* whose tangles

---

Le Dégagement multiple, Le Collet de Buffle, 1976

...refresh the eyes
against the abyss...

Network of fragmentary/fragmenting strength and *empty border bordering the void* (stands up *against*? *against the abyss*), in Laporte and in Eigner, two modes appear to undermine the continuity, the density of discourse, both (*both*) beginning from (*from*) the enigmatic *evidence* (word resembling — let's quickly say it *as a practical joke* — the perfect stencilo of (*emptiness*) of what can happen during the work of writing, i.e. the incoercible exfoliation of the blackened leaf, the *biographical (Life scatters its lesson)* documentary pulverization, where *"time changes at the opening of a new calendar."*

Here, delicately trapped by one of the most dramatic auto-designations, there, inscribed *with* anecdote itself and in the midst of its *marginal* suspension (*projective/fall forward*), the *new biography*, major biography, "this superexistence" asserts itself (without telling) be it by the transformation of its means of distribution, be it by the (endless) exploding of its text field, thus subverted...

How to read "this ellipse of history"?
these "forests of possibility"?
How to read these two (*projective*) celebrations of the weave, these conjugations of "vanishing lines" sustained by who knows what "fearful symmetry"?

Emmanuel Hocquard

This Story Is Mine:
Little Autobiographical Dictionary of Elegy

> *Pretty soon I heard whimpering.*
> James Durham, *Dark Window*

AH! ————————▶ ALAS!

The classical elegy, as it was taught to us (poem expressing regret, lament (V. *that word*), sadness, melancholy, pain, nostalgia, etc.) obeys the following schema: *it had begun well; time passed; and, in the end, it went bad.*

1st column: **Ah!**	*time passes*	2nd column: **Alas!**
I had some great times with Cynthia.	————▶	Today I am miserable because Cynthia is totally frivolous.
I was happy in Rome, surrounded by friends and covered in laurels.	————▶	Now I am all alone and sad in my exile in Romania.
Myrto shipped out, content to be on her way to marry in Camarine.	————▶	Alas, the ship sank, and Myrto drowned.

Cette histoire est la mienne, Notes (Ed. Raquel Levi), 1997

If Propertius and Ovid take us into their confidence, and Chenier on the other hand brings us tabloid news, in every instance it is a question of the lyric amplification of an anecdotal situation (V. **Anecdote**). And when, as at the piano, one presses all the way down on the hyperbolic pedal of elegiac representation, one achieves pathos.

To summarize: in the beginning, *tout va bien*. Then things spoil. Elegiac time flows in this direction: *Hélas pour moi!*

ANECDOTE

Tale related to a small fact of a private nature without universal implication. The elegist has a taste for anecdote. In fact, as far as he is concerned, everything is anecdote: digging a pond with friends (V. **Solitude**), building a chicken coop, or Hannibal's elephants and the delights of Capua.

    And even the anecdote that scares you
      it has currency no longer (spent, utterly spent)
with signs that say: here is the forest, and palace
    or port over there;

And above all, the anecdote that appalls you
    plunges head first
    into the sea

    There.
    Everything breaks through silence and sound
    this love and that Senate hearing.
and the rain along walls carved out of the rock.

    High rocks
    full, formed rocks
    of stone and earth and bone
    with words that pointed them out

    daily sedimentation.

BADURA SKODA

When he was young, pianist Paul Badura Skoda's playing charmed me, in some respects akin to Edwin Fischer's in terms of touch, but more muscular, in other respects close to Artur Schnabel's in its sustained notes but less incantatory.

Because of Badura Skoda, for a time I cherished the notion of becoming a pianist. The obstacle to this project was that ultimately I did not like music, which deadens vigilance. So I had to give up the idea of becoming a pianist, since I never could see how to play the piano without the music that went along with it.

Strangely, it was this very Paul Badura Skoda who found the answer to this dilemma, but long after (too late for me, alas) with his interpretation — his execution, I should say — of the *Hammer Klavier*.

Having had an exact replica of Beethoven's piano constructed, he followed the composer's advice to the letter: *play as if with a hammer*. In other words, hit the piano as if you are deaf. After playing the piece, you throw away the piano, since it has been destroyed.

Hearing the recording of this piece, I was impressed by the *tour de force*. And through it, since I thought I saw in Beethoven the project of giving music, to use Glenn Gould's expression, *its own opportunity to disappear*.

So I gave up on the piano and went for poetry with the intention of writing elegies. I am going to tell you how (V. *that word*).

BRECKELE

I'll tell you why I don't like onions.

Onions crystallize for me my first encounter with the abuse of power, with one of the first bids aimed at shattering my *joie de vivre*. At the time we were living on Dante Street, in Tangier. The apartment looked out onto the Strait. The kitchen faced east. Under the kitchen window there was a table. It was at this table that my grandmother made me eat breakfast each day, facing the sun, with no concern for my eyes which have always been very sensitive. Each day she put in front of me a big bowl of hot milk into which she poured the *breckele*.

Breckele are an Alsatian gastronomic specialty. To make *breckele*, take a loaf of black bread. From it cut a long slice thick enough to spread generously with slightly rancid butter. Place the buttered slice onto a cutting board. Take your large knife, dice the buttered bread. Dump it all into the bowl of scalding milk. Serve.

Up to this point, everything was going (almost) fine. *Hélas pour moi*, things spoiled quickly. Every morning, my day began with the revolting spectacle of cubes of buttered bread swelling and foundering in the hot liquid, while yellow eyes of melted butter began to float on the surface of the milk. But the worst was yet to come: you had to swallow this stuff down to the dregs before being allowed to leave the table. Now, the *breckele* tasted like onions. Every morning the *breckele* had the same taste of raw onions, because the knife or the cutting board (or both) had been used the night before, or even that morning, to chop onions.

Breckele is the **word** for: child-being blinded by sun, very hot and sweaty, gazing at butter eyes floating on the surface of a bowl of overheated milk, feeling his face coated with a fine greasy film, swallowing spongy bread that tastes of raw onion. Feeling very miserable. The *breckele* is elegiable (V. *that word*).

CAVE CANEM

Latin inscription in a mosaic depicting a dog at the entrance to the *House of the Tragic Poet* in Pompeii. It can be translated: *Beware of Dog.*

outside

REMEMBER

the ruins
the dry grass
the sun at three o'clock
fatigue
& the house of the tragic poet

CAVE CANEM

Examination of one's childhood unearths memories, so it is said. Not at all! Memories have never been the business of the past, they exist only in the present, in the moment and while *I remember*. Memories are words, phrases, spoken things. Not the past nor pieces of the past but language and pieces of language in the present. With his childhood memories, *the reverse elegist* (V. **Do, make**) reflects upon his language and not at all upon his little personal history which, in fact, has never taken place per se.

Sorting the tokens of "his past" on Montalban's table, he does not go backwards. He investigates in order to clarify a certain number of questions in the present. He is the sheep of which Panurges? He will forever resonate to what command words? He gyrates inside what meticulously restricted territories? What kind of grammar claims to govern his thoughts?

With only generalities to make, he has no choice but to begin with his own experience, *address his own circumstances* (V. **Breckele**).

"— What do you want from me? he asked, deadly earnest.
— Nothing but the story. The only thing that really interests detectives. To know exactly when all this hooey began to unfold.
— That's it?
I assured him that it ended there."

Contrary to the nostalgic elegist who proclaims his longing for the golden age, innocence and paradise lost, the *reverse elegist,* who loves to laugh, study and play, makes a deal, trading *ennui* and a serious spirit for play, work for study and sadness for delight.

COPY, COPYIST

When I was little — well, not that little — I copied whole books, or whole passages from books I loved, for my girl friend whom I loved. I could have sent her the books, but I sent her the copies, in my handwriting. My intention must have been to tell her I loved her by sending my handmade copies of books and passages from books that I loved.

DO, MAKE

Imagine a guy overflowing with good will, full of enthusiasm, and determined to proclaim his own current misery, starting with some good moments from his past. When he attends to this past, he can only find hideous reminders of anxiety, phobias, uncertainties. So how will he deal with it, absolutely determined to write elegies?

He tells himself,"I'll do what the others do, but backwards. I'm going to rifle through the trashcan of my past and the waste of history. With this miserable material, disparate and anecdotal, in other words, very *private*, I'll see what footage can be saved to edit. Yes, I'm an editor."

Starting from fragments (V. *that word*), signifying bursts from an insignificant quotidian, the *reverse elegist* will construct a montage, a piecemeal history, like his muse, the Brevet Brigadier General, Edgar Allan Poe's John A.B.C. Smith. When I say *construct*, Inspector, I mean — I am quoting — that this story is mine. The story of a *man that was used up*.

ELEGIABLE

Adj. (1987). According to Olivier Cadiot, worthy of figuring in an elegy. E.g.: *Gaby's potato pie.* (V. also **Breckele**).

"The list should also include
which kind of coffee
has such a satisfying taste"

Like saying
"This is how
I rank works of art"

For example waking this morning
J. heard a bird
whistle twice like a man

Or the plum tart

FRAGMENT

The *fragment* deserves our attention for a moment, if only by virtue of the fact that for some it causes a technical discomfort.

The life of the classical elegiac poet is a life *in the past* and a life *in the passive voice*. It has been shattered and the elegist, sighing, collects its fragments, odds and ends, bits and pieces.... These fragments represent for him what is left of a disappeared original state, one to which they recall him constantly. The elegiac poet rehashes and takes pleasure in it like the *Chinese dogs* "that gnaw on old bare white bones that haven't had any meat on them for a long time. But by gnawing them, they tear their gums and end up with the taste. The taste of their own blood."

To the eye of the *reverse elegiac* poet, whom one can also call the *tragic poet*, (V. **Cave canem**), the fragments don't reflect a disappeared origin or context or unity that would guarantee their meaning. What in the fragments fascinates him is not their causal link with events of his past life, but rather that they are so vivid they blow away all prior biographical context. They shine in the present with an unimaginable brilliance, with a brilliance of their own.

These decontextualized units — decontaminated, I should say — are floating propositions in the image of European currencies during a period of crisis: propositions returned to an autonomous state that no context need legitimate further and whose sole guarantee is my gaze, as though I am seeing them now for the first time.

I select them empirically (V. **Elegiable**) like the terms of a discrete series. George Oppen says, "...that there is a moment, an actual time, when you believe something to be true, and you construct a meaning from these moments of conviction."

These fragments do not link together but attract each other by "affinity," by a kind of necessity or ludic and happy intention, by *gay science*. When two fragments meet, their affiliation engenders a *kairos* (V. *that word*).

HOW

To write an elegy, you have to know how an elegy is made. And to find out how an elegy is made, treat it just like an engine. Choose a standard elegy, take it apart and study the separate pieces lying on the table.

Since the elegy has no particular form (you can give it one that suits you) nor fixed dimensions (it can be long, short or in between), you will look for what distinguishes it from other poetic genres. Now, scrutiny will reveal nothing in particular if not perhaps an above normal rate of *past tense*. It is, in fact, quite unusual to find verbs in the future tense in an elegy. And when there is one, it is generally in the form of a negative. E.g.: *I will never see you smile at me again.* The elegiac poet is a resolute pessimist.

After having looked closely at all the parts, put it back together, start up and listen to the engine hum. The difference is there. Elegy has a particular tone that distinguishes it from anything else, like the minor harmonics of clocks. The pitch of censure and resentment.

Thus, writing elegies is very simple. Read a lot of them (but not too many, because it is really quite depressing) and, if you have both ear and elegiac disposition, you're set.

It just takes care of itself. That's how I did it (V. **Do, make**).

IDENTITY

But *who's that crying?* "This story is mine" doesn't mean, as in the case of the classical elegists, that it is the representation of my inner life. The man that was used up has no inner life. Following the objectivist advice of Jean- Luc Godard, rather than expressing his impressions, he impresses his expressions. Literally (V. *that word*).

> make the list
> of dead leaves
>
> do not photograph falling
> leaves in
> morning mist
>
> *print* the list
> and *print* the word mist

> *print* this evening for dinner
> half a rabbit with carrots

When I say, Inspector — I quote — that *this life is mine*, I simply mean that I fabricate it. Like the author of *I remember*, I am the organizer of an anonymous intimate journal made from a list of anecdotes. *This life is mine* means: this is my list.

At times inexplicable things crop up on the list, enigmatic to others but also to me. Secrets (V. *that word*). Pure anecdotes remain secrets. Then what is really mysterious, says Pierre Alferi, is that this also can be shared. Or, *everybody's autobiography*. The man that was used up is without identity.

JOY WITHOUT HARM

The knot at the heart of it is the question of representation (represent or represent one's self). Heidegger, whom I do not like to quote, said, "thinking is presentifying, not representing."

The reverse elegist flees representation. Except in the sense of to copy (V. *that word*) literally (V. **Literal, literality, literally**). His activity is essentially ludic. Which does not necessarily mean comic. But he plays (V. **Childhood**). He plays with things as they exist (V. **Zukofsky**), with language as it exists (V. **Wittgenstein**). That is, as he meets them, before him and around him. Neither behind nor beneath him. He does not turn back, he does not dig. He gathers. His game consists of effecting (or not) unforeseen connections between the objects of language that present themselves, be they already representations (Cf. Reznikoff), which he treats as surfaces, for he is irreducibly superficial.

And when he achieves a good connection, a bold connection, he rejoices for a moment. Aristotle would speak of it as *a joy without harm*.

KAIROS

Amidst flowers: passionflowers

(and)

in the silent
chicken coop

even the dog's fleas
revive their appetite

now you

can scratch your tibia
entrancingly

violence of the gift
and innocence of the encounter

LAMENT

Orpheus turns. Euridice is lost to him.

And his lament rises into the void opened by what got away.

The classical elegist attempts to create a decoy by showering the void with regrets. Since his pain is too heavy to bear, he must share his secret (V. *that word*) with others. His lament can never fully describe his suffering.

For the *reverse elegist,* lament says language has no hold on what has escaped. His pain is unspeakable. So there is nothing to explain. No secret to share. His lament articulates the secret of an idiot.

In every case, the lament is the articulation of a secret.

> If, after all the comings and
> Goings, something so important
> Leaves such a persistent trace,
> How is it that you no longer have any idea
> What confuses you like this?

LITERAL, LITERALLY, LITERALITY

I am taking the word *literally* literally, *that is to say,* to the letter. Literality can only concern what arises from language (oral or written), *to the letter,* to the exclusion of propositions such as *Edward was literally mad* or *It literally happened like that,* where literally signifies something like really.

It follows that if one speaks of literality, one is talking about a proposition *already* formulated, orally or in writing, whatever be the truth of the phrase. For example, someone says: *Pascalle's dress is red.* It is quite clear to me that Pascalle's dress is green. But, if I repeat the articulated sentence, *Pascalle's dress is red,* I am literal. Literality is vertiginous, like the kind of double-barreled tautology it produces.

When I say that what I write is literal, I am not saying, then, that I'm making something out of anecdotes I've lived (even if it's the case); I simply mean that my articulations are intended to be taken to the letter, as they are reproduced in black and white. All my books are to be read as copies. I am the copier of my books (V. **Robinson Method**).

So

       the library was rebuilt
       (nice trompe-l'oeil effect)

          He composed black figures on a white ground
          little illuminated panels
          to Juno, to Janus, to Hope

ROBINSON METHOD

When Crusoe landed on his island after the shipwreck, he was not yet Robinson. He would be Robinson from the moment that, finding neither pen nor pencil in the jetsam, he liberated a cutter and some books. From these found objects would be born the method that names him.

Robinson speaks alone (V. **Solitude**), in words he learned while he was still just Crusoe, words he arranges as memories, that is, as objects of memory-language. Robinson on his island acts like Crusoe before the shipwreck but makes the same thing resonate differently.

The island is elegiable. Cut off from the world, with the fated means that are his, Robinson will reproduce Crusoe's world. He is a copier. And every copier, even the little classroom copier ripping off his desk partner, is an islander. Olivier Cadiot's *Future, ancient, fugitive* is, just like Perec's *I remember*, a splendid elegy.

SECRET

"What secret, Helena?"

"It's a secret."

That means: "Even I don't know." So a secret is first of all *my* secret. *My* secret does not mean: something I know, that I hide or that I reveal. *My* secret means something escapes *me*.

"The object" of my lament (V. *that word*) is my secret. And my lament exceeds the limits of my language, to the bounds of what separates my language from my non-language.

　　　　I speak through tears. In anger. "The outside! The with-out-language!"

Since "the object" of my lament is outside language, my lament is limited to a whimper, a scream, to the unarticulated. To animality: withdrawn into the least accessible regions of Thrace, Orpheus seeks only the company of wild animals.

　　　(What? Surely not a
scholiast but

　　　　　　a forest dweller
　　　　　　alone
　　　　　　in the bush

　　　　　　no matter what nonsense

　　　　　　of screaming
　　　　　　having the habit
　　　　　　　　　　　.)

SOLITUDE

Among all the poets, the elegist is the greatest consumer of solitude. The classical elegist deplores it; the *reverse elegist* considers it the unique opportunity *a)* to get away from platitude; *b)* to see in platitude something other than platitude. For example, the *Canale*.

The *Canale* is a pond 6 project. A white trapezoid drawn in the grass in powdered chalk, when seen through the camera's optics, appears as a perfect square (photographs have been taken); which, seen by the naked eye from the stone placed in pond 3, appears to be a perfect rectangle.

In order to see the *Canale* as a perfect rectangle, I must position myself standing on the stone at the water's surface. *You* too can see it <u>as</u> I see it, if you come stand where I am on the same stone. Then you see it and then you can say, <u>like me</u>, "*I* see it."

The stone in the water (an island) placed in pond 3 is the *only* vantage point from which *I* or *you* can see the white trapezoid as a perfect rectangle. But to see it you have to go there yourself. When I see it I can say that I see it but I can not make visible what I see. No possible representation exists of what I *alone* see "by direct observation" from my island. I can only describe it as precisely as possible. My description is a guide. A guide to my solitude.

"*I am frightened* can for example be said simply to explain my actions. But these words are far from groans, they can even be said with a smile."

"The words *I am in pain* can be a lament and can also be something else."

"For why is the lament *I am in pain* different from the simple fact? Of course because of its intention. And that can express itself by means of the tone."

"*I must tell you: I am frightened.*"
"*I must tell you: it makes me shiver.*"
"And one can say this in a <u>smiling</u> tone of voice too."

"...there isn't any word you can't use if you have enough body to make something of it.... What I mean is the kind of thing you get in Chapman's 'the unspeakable good liquor there.' Obviously, the man who wrote that knew what it was to gargle something down his throat."

Roger Laporte

Loose Leaf

You must be resolutely modern.
Keep the ground gained.
Rimbaud

for Anne-Marie Albiach & Claude Royet-Journoud

I have accepted the rules of the game: to write a single page! Volume thus reduced, radically flattened, unmasks a temptation to which I will give in: to write a program, a manifesto or better still a will.

1) Even if we were to name the artists, few in number, who, though belonging to their time, were first of all our contemporaries, in fact our precursors; even if inadvertently our books were shelved in the Library, if they were entered under the rubric WRITING in the catalogue of Schools of Literature, our texts would not belong to Literature. How to note this *difference*?

2) We mean not only to engineer a transformation analogous to that of abstract painting in relation to figurative, but we expect mutation, we will instigate the emergence of a new *element: to write*, so vital that Kafka, in a letter from 5-7-22, confided to Max Brod, "The existence of a writer really depends on his desk; in fact, he is never permitted to leave it."

Feuille volante, Le Collet de Buffle, 1986

3) The live-write relationship must be reversed: Rousseau reduplicates his life drafting his "Confessions" whereas a man's life, his social life, must reduplicate, expand, or at least receive this *writing* by which it will be "changed" (which would be impossible if *to write* were not to stage an *other* life).

4) One who writes belongs to this *different* world, since in exploring its multiple shifting dimensions he is also in search of himself, and yet he remains lost, not to be found. But this inhospitable earth, would it not be the wilderness that is home to a nomad?

5) To those tempted to respond YES to the petition on this page, we guarantee a life, so *exhilarating* in spite of all, they will never have any real longing for ordinary life: we promise them work, work so beyond measure that they die before really having begun; for them we predict the secret glory of a useless passion, a life so cruel they will run out of tears, excessive endless wearing out of all their strength, a poverty that never belies itself, since what attempts to distract or hide is endlessly scattered by the wind on the way.

Is it necessary to add? If this task could be accomplished by one person, this page would not have been written.

1972

Roger Laporte

Letter to Claude Royet-Journoud

24 Dec. 1985

Dear Claude,

will I manage to write you this letter I promised? I don't know. Live talk would doubtless be more favorable. — I put down the "Rötring 2000," choosing instead my "Olivetti Praxis 20": the impersonality of the keyboard gives me a little distance, space, which settles to some degree what is too violent, too raw in my confidences. — I'll try to be brief, to summarize my "impressions from reading," certainly very subjective, in a report.

Concerning "La Veille": I think I've already written you that the language wasn't yet formed, it isn't yet what it should have been, and I was not in the state of mind, even if that's normal, to bring such a project to completion. — That said, it took some nerve, I think, to write such an unprecedented book.

"Une voix de fin silence": the most I have to say about it is that the one who wrote that book has become a complete stranger to me. I am not at all able to re-inhabit, even in an imaginary way, who I was. Only about a dozen pages (on sobriety) still affect me. "Pourquoi," the end of this book, is in fact a complete failure, precisely because I do not actually say it, admit it. Only my bitter tone witnesses my final failure.

---

fig., No. 1 (1989)

"Fugue," the "Fugue project," so long (1968-1975). The 6th sequence isn't bad; the very last pages of the 9th sequence reasonably successful*; in "Supplément" there's a page here and there that's still readable, but generally speaking, and before tempering my judgment, I'd say I seriously wonder who'd really be interested in such a CRAZY project (again, I could not be speaking more seriously), not just crazy but hairsplitting, irritating and even at times tedious (forgive me for speaking so brutally about your friend Roger Laporte's work).

And yet I at least credit myself for having taken it to the limit. But it cost me. I remember very well (but I won't dwell on it) that around '75 I had, let's say tactfully, some psych problems. Briefly, although here it's almost impossible to be brief, on the one hand, my judgment is hypercritical. But on the other, it can't truly be, to the extent that in "Fugue" a kind of rigorous, pitiless logic takes shape, cruel even (in Artaud's sense of the word) that later in the pursuit will be so many trumps. On the other hand, this defeat, exhaustion, weakness allowed me to *be written*. That's how I read the "Codicille," which I realize continues in the first three sequences of "Suite" — (but from a certain moment that I could almost locate it is really "Suite," which is to say MORIENDO). In the end, the verdict to apply to "Fugue" (the project) is of necessity ambiguous and must be circumspect. Basically, for myself, I am prompted to say this: it was the path, sure enough, and it might well be that the path will never be a rosy one but will remain dry, irritating, thoroughly unproductive. Even to that part of my work you can apply Cid Corman's famous formula: *"The one way is the hard way."* Could I have done otherwise, that is, gone another way? There's no answer to such an empty question.

As for "Suite" MORIENDO, I won't talk about it. Even to a very close friend, it's easier to say all the bad things one thinks about one's work than to say...I will just say at certain moments reading "Fugue" I was really in despair, but "Moriendo"

---

*I'm ungrateful: I'm forgetting the first paragraph of the 1st sequence!

consoled me. You are in a good position to know what, for example, Cid Corman thinks of it (I'm not forgetting that I owe this translator and friend to you): assuming there are a scant dozen people (to this day) thinking like him. — And another thing: even someone who can't read what is written right in the *post-scriptum* (it took me months!) can't not understand that it is impossible to go beyond these 615 pages.

Since we are friends and writers, perhaps you will allow this letter, strange as it is, this letter at least in part quite painful, in any case a completely confidential letter, to be the Christmas gift Roger Laporte gives Claude Royet-Journoud.

And I am already sending my

BEST WISHES FOR 1986

love,

Roger

P.S.
    1 I would like to have written a single book, "Moriendo" (which would begin around the 4th or 5th sequence of *Suite* and finish at the p.s. of "Moriendo.")
    2 Don't misunderstand: I haven't forgotten that the last sequence has not been and can not be written, which uniquely relativizes any success, inappropriate word in any case.
    3 So I would like to have written just "Moriendo," plus some etudes, especially "B v V" (I liked the color of the of the 1st edition's cover better).

Roger Lewinter

Letter to Claude Royet-Journoud

Claude,

...I'm out on strike, "literally and in every sense." Why?
The exclusion of myself from *L'attrait des choses* has created a state
of deprivation. I know it is that way after every book, but there,
insofar as I was seeking to capture the structure of my thinking
(my being in the world), which placed me in relation to things, to
works, to beings, now I suddenly feel deprived of all relation
with those things, those works, those beings, and also, as a result,
of myself, precisely insofar as these things, these works, these
beings filling me, inhabiting me, provoked a response, made a
place, by means of my response, for dialogue, placed me in relation to myself. I am outside myself, in the real sense but not in the
'ecstatic' sense (not emptiness but vacuum), without the structure
of conversation which also and above all engenders fiction (dream
as representation of the future: opening to the horizon to project,
express, articulate towards). This state is without doubt
'drought.' I do not see or no longer see (for the moment) what I
can anticipate, since everything works by that leap of the heart
now missing. Dispossession is surely this: absence of the internal
interpellation ('no longer knowing how to pray'). And in a certain
way, for the first time, this deprivation of the heart's magnetic
force fills me with fear. I am deprived of (my) interior net which,
surrounding me — holding me — allowed me to be a wakeful
sleeper: to sleepwalk outside in safety.... With no idea of waiting,
I must continue without knowing how to continue, in a time

L'in-Plano, No. 52 (1986)

which is no longer a present, since it is without a past and with-out a future plan. Simply dis/continued: or, continuing to be, I have the impression of playing, i.e., of repeating myself: pacing in a place that no longer has the space to be. The only reason to go on would be God, whom I do not dare to address, since that means love and I am presently without what gives elan — heart — to address it, being loveless.... So, the experience I wanted — which ordered *L'attrait des choses* for me — was exactly to arrive at being freed from the past as unspoken intimacy, unfastened from my personal involvement, surrendered into the wait for grace, which is no longer worthwhile....

As for my desire for an echo of *L'attrait des choses* — that people speak to me about it — and the strange frustration I feel when people speak to me about it — the feeling of insatiability about it, that it is never it. And when, by happenstance, it is it, a sort of despair — now I realize that it is connected to this: what can be said about it only confirms for me that I can no longer feel it. And since it was me, that I am no longer my living self — since it's not, in this case, autobiography which can be pursued inde-finitely, but a novel from which the author is cut loose, exiled, as soon as he has finished it, and where it is inconceivable that he can begin to live again once he has brought it to term. People talk to me about what I have killed — jubilation at the moment when the 'subject' appeared before me, when I felt the trap in place around me had snapped shut; that, having so long been the stalker in hiding, I finally had caught, unable ever to escape, myself. To live otherwise. And now I am simply declaring that the breathing of others cannot revive me, nor can I make myself live as before the book.

Maybe it's there, that game of passe-passe where one discovers that "art is swill".... And yet.

Roger Lewinter

Roger Lewinter

Report

The text I am working on will surely amount to about thirty pages when I am done -seventeen have already been written-, not counting a brief prologue, will consist of one single unbroken sentence where the rules of syntax are applied, grammatically and logically, so as not to use a period; this to translate formally the continuity of feeling of which this text is the telling; but especially to restore the process of mental life which wants to capture whatever events are taking place, to combine them into a fabric, ultimately coherent.

The avoidance of the period, in the measure to which it carries the suspension of the principal statement, whose hierarchy of meaning ordinarily informs the course of the sentence -determining the number and function of different subordinates, where the motive of its utterance, insofar as it is anticipated, is made explicit- foregrounds the narrative -logical- problem that atonal music had encountered in its time: to imagine an organizing principle which would no longer, in its completion, be the result of a preliminary propositional -melodic- structure, foreign to the words forced to reproduce it in their arrangement but without the sentence confining itself by these very means to the camouflaged juxtaposition of independent elements -words which, detached from their subjective referential frame of the sentence, are absolute signs for things.

More precisely: in the measure to which, in French, the principal-subordinates order of the propositions is prefigured in the subject-verb-attribute sequence of the words, it can not be abolished without being reversed, systematizing, in order to implement it, the hyperbaton -inversion or disjunction of the normal word order- which, by the different discursive distribution it sets up, naturally allowing for the parenthetical clause, creates a narrative polyphonic space : where the tale, in its linear progression, is perception of a voice separating itself by conjectural combination from the others that coexist.

Moreover, two formal elements which appeared to be bound to the exercise of poetry have asserted themselves progressively: rhyme -between two words of different purpose, no more concrete : identity of sound, partial but abstract : partial convergence of meaning-, effecting notably the transition between the end of a parenthetical clause and the recovery of a statement; and, in the absence of the principal, which, focusing attention on the development of the argument, renders it secondary, a relation of regular length among the different propositional segments, structuring itself metrically.

The present text would like to bring to term the project sketched in *The Attraction of Things* -composed of sentence-paragraphs- and *The History of Love in Solitude* -containing a one-sentence tale, mirrored fugue- : since it is now resisted in poetry -yet is the foundation of any legitimate writing- to articulate in prose that regularity which, conferring on language an aesthetic coherence that liberates the work from the arbitrariness of the author, in its play objectifies transcendence.

Raquel

Alba
Suite after an anonymous text

I

The leaves one against the other, the book is closed. Only resemblance of borders occurs. *A hand lets the day enter.*

Action poétique, No. 75 (1978)

II

The dawn unwinds. The borders overtake the surfaces. Under the pages the volume whitens. *What I have left.*

III

The coming day works at the loss of color,
of my love. Between a black thread and a
white thread, my voice does not carry *the
song of the canvas* any further.

IV

Also there is the question of the wind that
arrives from afar. Of the light on what
color remains.
I am beautiful. *You are like me.*

Mitsou Ronat

Mental Burn*

A pain   *the eternal glorious wound*
A book   *which to poetry*   **Name-Work**
crossing pure mental experience, in order to read it.
          or mystery of being already expressed
it must be imagined, closed — folded, or put down.
          thought was crossing roles
To make abstraction   *even if close to silence* —   of all vision
yet there   **when the body is a sentence to come,** preliminary,
necessary to the pulse
yes, he pressed authentic lips for a new gush

                    the hand taken in the page
in response to fright : state of reversed name of the goddess,
some gray lines, dense or diffuse or : flayed
                    genuine mental prints, or even
                              VOCAL
          BE HOLD, voices in registers, visible voices
on magnetic tapes,
          giving in return the sound of tongues
                              by the action of light
          the dark body in which the name is lodged...

Orange Export Bulletin, No. 5 (June 1976)
*Claude Royet-Journoud/Lars Fredrikson, *Le Travail du nom,* Maeght
Editeur, 1976, Collection "Argile."

Mitsou Ronat

*The ONE of Language**

Messages of death reach cities one may reach by water — from
Venice to Troy, the secret threads of a 'carnival' of languages cut
through flesh bound by friendship

> Threads stretch between the points, the angles
> extend. One breaks down and one seeks all means of
> agreement

Through their rifts, *récits** similar to the lovers of G. B., let a poison
infiltrate, from one to an other, even before having been spoken
and without arrangement

(a language tired of walking, on the side
testing the desire thereof)
open the passage to the neutral: he

> saying I in all innocence or by pure linguistic con-
> vention

transforming the alternation of people in dialogue and people
seen as the single and massive person who in reality makes history

the one of language
owed to Ulysses by Nemo, his person, his question
in French   can *one*   say
Oscillation of sex, 'fluttering' of looks, mad trick of attributions*,
bringing to light the INDEFINITE — the confused

Change, No. 18 (1974)
* This montage is made up of quotations from *Dire I* (Danielle Collobert), *Les
Troyens* (J.-P. Faye), *Melencolia* (J.-C. Montel), and a commentary.

What can we do now, you and I joined beneath the
same face with absence on the inside...
In vain have I tried a separation, to each a separate
history

For between you and me, *one* could not distinguish the sex
   (certain texts reading in the dark) even in the shadows of a
low   lamp
For language offers its circumspect partitions or its malignant
borders (shamming precision), disarmed as soon as *one* questions it
       E V ?
                No, EL, simply. E and L : it's quickly done.
                He objects: But in my country that means *him*.
So, underneath the particles that *one* (of language — *that* tyrant of
the *I*) would call determined, THAT (other), *that one (f.)* or *that one
(m.)*, pulses a multitude of distended dislocated bodies which,
approaching, change volume
   (at the risk of making a liar of Spinoza) among them, furtive
imperceptible relations, or falsely
           a n d t h u s c o n t e m p l a t i n g t h e h i s t o r y
           h e c a n n o t t e l l where he only sees himself, by
           hundreds (or thousands)
There in the writing — the illusory person still speaks ironically:
on that claim of naming *That* (young man), pointed at but absent
from roll call, whose identity vanishes with his origin
              And your name, it's what?
           Nar. *One* does not know where that came from.
At the moment when *one*, unthinkable, but inevitable subject,
gives its meaning to syntax
   (language comes undone hearing you in it) the indefinite
moves in, under the definite, provisionally governing infinitive
and noun
           To enter, to dissolve there, to move through
           passages, to lodge in cranes to go up and down
           impacts against the buildings of blackened brick,
           explosion, *one* abridges in the concrete
of history

(THAT hero AT THE POINT OF DEATH) no longer to be pointed out

(Propositions)

— The transformation of pronouns, the annulment of the sexes in the *one* by means of the permutation of persons, plays the death of psychological myth: the being is dissolved in the lattice of languages...

— If *one* was born with man, it is in order to do without the concept. Far from being an "at your service" (of art) or a neutrality (of classification). The new function of the *one* appears in the gaps in those *récits* where the theory of history surreptitiously recovers the fiction from which it was born.

Jacques Roubaud

"scream or like burns never said"

> Danielle Collobert:
> *Meurtre*   Gallimard, 1964, 144 pp.
> *Dire I-II*   Laffont, 1972, 194 pp., Coll. "Change"
> *Il donc*   Laffont, 1976, 126 pp., Coll. "Change"
> *Survie*   Orange Export, 1978, 16 p.

In time, for her, prose, in a reverse of today's accustomed direction, became poetry. But as, for her, the prose of the tale was born of a death, of an impossibility of poetry, it is from the death of the tale that later, for her, poetry came once again. It is almost impossible to separate it, today, from her death.

"I can't do it," she said, "poetry. I don't know what it is." But at the end, suffocating in prose, at the end of sentences. "With poetry," she said, "what I write has only a resemblance." Simply not to be able to go to the typographic end of the lines any more. To have to interrupt them. Not intentionally, by suffocation. Not to occupy the page. To settle in its blanks, its silences. In *what is left when nothing more is necessary — punctuation — linkage.*

There is quite enough silence like that. Involuntary poetry, because *no more to say.* Ends of speech pushed by the infinitive. "You won't hold it against me, telling you. I don't know poetry."

Critique, No. 385/6 (June-July 1979)

Thus for her in the past, beginning with the tale, poetry having to be forever denied: *this meeting with the inner eye, behind the keyhole, that sees, and that finds the outer eye caught in the act of seeing, of curiosity, of uncertainty.* She told the tale of instants. Made *the minuscule parasites come out of the wood, so old, its very patina looked innocent.* But behind the parabolas generated by certain axioms of impossibility, (of face, of name, of road), behind the confusion of an "I" hounded by its ordinary and grammatical signals of identity, not really singular nor plural, nor masculine, feminine, something waits fourteen years to speak out against *identical neutrality of the abyss,* as if the mute double of this prose had long been preparing to meet the unverifiable, death.

I can no longer say my name.
And I must protect myself. Against everything. I cohere with the morning people.
I don't know what to do, what road to take.
Each day I take the form of a departure. There are no preparations to make. I just decide. I get up where I find myself, I cross the city's whole breadth. I reach the suburbs. I have to go further, along gray walls, glaucous water, blackened fences.
I have become accustomed to living at night. The beginning of night always brings me a strange kind of serenity.
I have the sense of living a death.
I say end, I say it's the end, really finished this time. I will say no more, I will no longer repeat endlessly. I am in the totally black room, all dark with thick night; because I always hope for that thickness, but rarely the world. She pushes a door. There is a light somewhere, very faint. She goes up. I am below. I wait. It's settled. Then I go up too. I am out of breath, I think. The door is open. She is on the bed, in a raincoat, eyes staring. I look at her. I have to leave. She's dead.

Later, pushed ceaselessly down that road, from poetry towards the impossibility of poetry, from the impossibility of personal poetry to impersonal prose towards the tale of the impersonalization of prose, whence she came, in some moment of plenitude in this renunciation, in a pause in the road of erasure, to the surprise of a precarious balance (*precise details leading to the tale of uncertain moments*) where there seemed to be simultaneously a "you" and an "I," for some possible duplicity facing the truncating silence.

You shivered in my hands and I freeze the shivering here. Sitting very close for a long time on the riverbank, broad and calm under the sun, redness of the banks, for a long time in the reflections, the quick tracings, the passage of things in water.
Dazzling. Air so soft, light clouds, stratified in the deserted plane.
Simple articulation, end of words, of effort, a sound enveloped by its own echo — the resistance of a wave upon another — undulation to infinity.
Lull.

Then comes the story of dissolution. Each paragraph takes the form of a departure. There are no preparations to make. Language alone decides. The sentence stands up where it is (materially, anywhere in the world. It was there.) It crosses the whole breadth of the page. And can go no further.

To stay there with the word — for a long time — looking all around — waiting
Day that passes — perhaps — always here — darkness —around the word — always the single sound — same note held dully — ceaselessly.

The words stop it.

extinction of images
no more fitting together the fragments
                    — opaque chains
choice
no more choice

So, as in proportion *time — the invariable* of prose, even *transcribed* no longer consoled for the immobility, with time, for her, this form not verse had become inseparable from the speech of identity she wanted abolished, and by the slowing down of sentences seized with intensity and abstraction, she found again after every digression the same circular trap, the gag of lyric in the mouth, that *outside of which / is neither speaking nor language./*

That is why at the last moment the six poems of *Survie* contradict (wildly plural), because from all "elsewhere" only a *generalized what good is it* has come back.

I speech mouth opening open to say I live to whom
because at the end, again "she-I opens a door. she-I go up. It's settled. She-I is on the bed, in a raincoat, eyes staring. I-she look at her for a while. I-she-I is dead."

Because "the inner eye" has, finally, met "the outer eye."

I leaving voice without response articulating sometimes words
that silence response to other ear never
if to muteness world not a sound
plunges into blue cosmos

enough enough
exit

Jacques Roubaud

La fleur inverse

I am of Provençal origin. The Provençal language, which I did not speak as a child, which today I read but do not speak, plays an essential role in my family memory: at once close and absent, it is for me the language of origin, the lost language of the golden age of poetry, in the perfumed garden of languages of which Dante speaks. French, my mother tongue and my language of thought and of work, is for that reason my language of exile.

Writing poems, composing poetry in contemporary conditions, is a difficult exercise. Persisting on this path assumes the choice of a model, the reference to a favorite period, where poetry existed and shone. I have chosen XIIth century Provence. Poetry can be thought of through the Troubadours, their example. The most contemporary poetry, in order to survive, must defend itself from erasure, from oblivion, from disdain, by the choice of an archaism. My archaism is the *trobar*.

The idea of poetry as art, as craft, and as passion, as play, as irony, as research, as knowledge, as violence, as autonomous activity, as life form, this was the idea for many poets. I see its first example in the Troubadours.

So this book is an homage, and indirectly speaks of the poetry of our time.

Editions Ramsay, 1986

Jacques Roubaud

American Poetry

Édition Gallimard's request for an anthology of American (USA) poetry in 1972 (completed by 1975 but not yet* published for various reasons) involved me in a rather systematic reading of what had appeared in that language ("American English") since Pound, Williams, cummings and Stevens, outside of "the Beat Generation." It was a revelation to me. Groups such as the *Objectivists* (Zukofsky, Reznikoff, Oppen, Rakosi), *Black Mountain* (Olson, Creeley, Blackburn), the *New York School* (Ashbury, Schuyler, Mathews, O'Hara), all practically unknown here, bore witness to a very great wealth, originality, freedom of "the golden age" of American poetry. I discovered *Origin,* Cid Corman's magazine, Eshleman's *Caterpillar* and the work of Jack Spicer. John Cage, MacLow, Rothenberg and David Antin, and many others. The reigning verse practice made French vers libre seem to me limited in comparison, constrained, fearful, stiff and hesitant. I collected some of my "readings" in an issue of *Action poétique* (Zukofsky, Rothenberg, Antin, Padgett, Corman, MacLow especially, translated by J. Guglielmi and myself), and *Change* published the three major Spicer "books": *Billy the Kid, The Holy Grail, Language.*

---

*Mezura, No. 9 (1979)

[Jacques Roubaud writes this in 1979; the anthology, *Vingt poètes américains,* appears in 1980.]

Jacques Roubaud

from: *Poésie, etcetera: ménage*

2 — Nations, Poetry

At times, in some countries, distant or near, someone asks, "Is there a French poetry?"

(meaning, "Is there still poetry in France?" (meaning, "You know very well (your newspapers themselves are full of it), there is no more literature in France. And you're French! And you call yourself a poet! How do you explain this?) — what could I answer? I don't answer at all)

More generally, if X is a country, what does "the poetry of X" mean?

3 — Eine Nationale Poesie?

@1

@1.1 In my family, the telephone made no inroad until 1945. I was twelve. It was a strange and formidable apparatus, a kind of divinity, undoubtedly hostile. My father did not wish to answer its call, even less to initiate its use. It was my mother's job to exorcise it. But even she must not have really succeeded in mastering it. In fact, several years having gone by, we had left Carcassonne where we had lived for the entire war (let me remind you that there was a war from 1939 to 1945), we had come to Paris to live

Stock, 1995

and one day my mother received a phone call from an old friend from back there, from before. They spoke for a moment, exchanged news about family, children, and when they were about to hang up my mother said, "Let's not let so much time go by without speaking. Take my telephone number." "Yes, you're right, give it to me," the friend began to say. At that moment they both broke into laughter.

@1.2 As for myself, I have not progressed very much in the mastery of this instrument. And, when I received a call from Hamburg asking me the title for my talk for today, I had a moment of panic. Thinking of the unbelievable distance traveled by the voice arriving invisibily at my ear, I answered bluntly, with hesitation in voice and ear, "a national poetry?" And so this is how the title occurred to me, practically illiterate in German matters, in a kind of German, something I find well adapted; and thus subsequently I adopt "Eine nationale Poesie?" pronouncing it my way.

@1.3 I will proceed in the following manner. First I will question the idea of nation. Secondly I will ask myself what poetry can have to do with nation. I will stay more or less in an interrogatory mode, having few answers to bring forward; which will not prevent me from expressing myself peremptorily, like everyone else.

@2
@2.1 For some years, France, eager to indicate it harbors no ill will towards Germany for certain misunderstandings arisen in their recent common history, has borrowed their concept of a political movement with fascist tendencies called the Front National whose leader (there has to be a leader) is named Le Pen.

@2.2 One of the strong ideas of the Front National is "France for the French!" or "Stick together and our cows will be kept safe!" There are too many foreigners in France, they say, they are invading us, like the Arabs long ago, conquered by Charles Martel (an honorary member of the Front National) in Poitiers in 732. They eat our bread, break into our security and our social security. In short, "They leap into our arms / massacre our children and our mates." At least symbolically.

@2.3 So we must get rid of the foreigners.

@2.4 At this moment we encounter a problem. If we send these foreigners back to their homeland, it means we can distinguish them in a clear and indisputable way from the French, who must remain home. Good. What is a French person?

@2.5 Laboring over the question, the Front National, in the voice of its leader (there has to be a leader speaking in everyone's name) has proposed a definition of a French person.

@2.6 <u>Le Pen's Definition</u>: **He or she whose parents are both French is French.**

@2.7 Enthusiastic about this definition, I composed the following poem, already translated into a number of languages, I say proudly (this does not happen to me very often), including German.

@2.8 Attention: the poem must be read very fast!

@2.9. Poem:

Is Le Pen French?

If Le Pen were French according to Le Pen's definition, that would mean that, according to Le Pen's definition, Le Pen's mother and Le Pen's father would have been themselves French according to Le Pen's definition, which would mean that, according to Le Pen's definition, Le Pen's mother's mother, as well as Le Pen's mother's father as well as Le Pen's father's mother not to forget Le Pen's father's father would have been, according to Le Pen's definition, French, and it follows that Le Pen's mother's mother's mother as well as that of Le Pen's mother's father as well as that of Le Pen's father's mother, and that of Le Pen's fathe's father would have been French according to Le Pen's definition; and by the same token, and for the same reason, Le Pen's mother's mother's father, as well as that of Le Pen's mother's father as well as that of Le Pen's father's mother, and that of Le Pen's father's father would have been French, always according to the same definition, that of Le Pen

whence one will deduce with no trouble and without the help of Le Pen, following this reasoning

either there is an infinite number of French people who were born French according to Le Pen's definition, who lived and died French according to Le Pen's definition since the dawn of the beginning of time or else

Le Pen is not French according to Le Pen's definition.

Jacques Roubaud, Provençalß

@2.10 I had to sign "Provençal," not being French myself but more or less Provençal, in any case I am if you go back a few generations. (I would gladly place the troubadour Rubaut among my ancestors, but I have not succeeded in determining as yet all the missing links in my genealogy.)

@2.11 The second branch of the alternative, namely that Le Pen is not French according to his own definition received stunning confirmation recently. While in New York for a reading at the Poetry Project at Saint Mark's Place, and after I read my poem, someone brought me a pen with the brand name Le Pen. Examining it I saw that it was "made in Japan." Quod erat demonstrandum .

57 — On the Avant-gardist Gesture

—The avant-gardist stance, you tell me, is manifest above all in gestures. You speak of the avant-gardist gesture.

—The avant-garde, in effect, is easily the "youth garde."

—"Youth garde?"

—I am thinking of a song from the twenties: "Look out/You bourgeois, you pigs/the youth garde's/a-comin' down the street..."

—Now you're being ironic.

—No. It's clear that the avant-gardist gesture is necessary. Against the aging, static, fixed tradition, the avant-gardist gesture of destruction is necessary.

—Yeah, so?

—So, accompanied by the *tabula rasa* slogan (absolute destruction and reconstruction starting from nothing, "down with this world I'll build a better one") it is largely illusory.

—Some reasons, examples of these difficulties?

—The avant-gardist gesture is condemned to repetition. Very quickly becomes psittacist. It can't avoid repeating itself. Or disappearing.

The avant-gardist gesture: the repetition compulsion of the dream of destroying the repetitive mechanics of tradition.

The avant-gardist gesture is a gesture of destruction-liberation. But

The liberating gesture masks the poverty of the *tabula rasa* gesture.

The avant-gardist gesture treats tradition with derision, with violence. This derision, this violence are necessary in order that the destruction be effective. But doing this caricatures tradition. It isn't taken seriously. It is attacked through its symptoms, its most superficial characteristics (the ones that are the very indications of its degeneration). And it must be thus. For if the avant-gardist gesture stops for a second to consider tradition in a serious way, it might as well leave its weapons at the door. It loses all destructive force. The avant-gardist gesture never gets out of this contradiction.

—Well why not?

—Because in fact tradition isn't destroyed like that. There is no possible firing squad for poetic tradition. There is no possible eradication of it. "Quaint poetics," the out-of-date, used up, antiquated traditional forms survive underneath, as soon as the avant-gardist gesture is faced with duration.

Amnesia has never been a good thing, even and especially for revolutionaries. *Tabula rasa* is not an effective weapon against the weight of the past. It is practically impossible barring a very radical attempt, the success of which is never guaranteed (ghosts remain, at the very least).

Now the allegedly destroyed forms survive, particularly in the memory of avant-gardist poetry itself.

So, in poetry, the *tabula rasa* strategy has ironic effects of return, of which the Surrealists' "standard French *vers libre*"is a typical case (I have studied this situation in detail in a book, *La Vieillesse d'Alexandre*).

Moreover, in what concerns the products proper to the avant-garde, in the face of a fixed norm, the gesture of placing itself outside the norm does not guarantee that the poem will equal its own norm, its elan.

But there is yet another difficulty. The avant-gardist gesture is exposed to the temptation of revolutionary advance flight which is revolution in politics. Doesn't changing "the verse line" participate in changing society? Isn't reforming "the verse line" being a reformer? Doesn't destruction of the verse line, an expression of the society needing to be destroyed, participate in the destruction of this society?

The later version is quite a comical form: to practice the avant-garde gesture in art is to be revolutionary, is to put society in question. (The Surrealists themselves, with greater caution, proposed Surrealism and the surrealist revolution at the service of the revolution).

The avant-gardist advance flight can also be counter-revolution-ary: Pound, Céline, Benn. The avant-gardists become post-moderns easily recognize themselves in them.

—If I understand correctly, the avant-gardist gesture exhausts itself, and very quickly.

—Its virtue, which is to face down the intolerable out-dated forms of tradition, if it is to act, acts very swiftly. That's Dada.

Otherwise, the avant-gardist gesture quickly disappoints the avant-gardists. Because it seems to them that they have gone nowhere.

The "return to" is one of the possible consequences of the depletion of the avant-gardist gesture.

The natural outcome of the avant-gardist gesture is, in fact, silence.

Let us recall that the glorious version of modernist avant-gardist gesture, with Rimbaud, transforms into trafficking.

Verse liberators get old and become verse slavers.

Each avant-gardist gesture is bound to fail if it is not accompanied by formal understanding. But the avant-gardist has no time for understanding.

—And now?

Avant-gardism was linked to the modernist moment.

The avant-gardism of the postmodern moment is to announce the end of avant-gardes.

58 — An example

—A particularly striking example of the repetition effect, of the psittacism of the avant-gardist gesture is comic in nature.

—You are kidnapping Marx's dictum about the moment of tragedy and the moment of farce (repetition).

—It's true that repetition is one of the great weapons of the comic.

—And your example?

—Tel Quel. The Tel Quel group.

The Tel Quel group was the Surrealist Movement's farce.

59 — What!

"What! Because we had Napoléon-le-Grand, do we have to have Napoléon-le-Petit?" (Victor Hugo)

What! Because we had Breton, did we have to have Breton-le-Petit!

Agnès Rouzier

from *Letters to a Dead Writer*

There is death in life and it astonishes me that people pretend not to know that: death whose pitiless presence we feel in each change we survive, for one must learn how to die slowly. We must learn how to die: there's our whole life.

I am not ashamed, Dear, to have wept, another Sunday, cold and too early, in the gondola that kept turning and turning, passing vaguely outlined neighborhoods that seemed to me to belong to another Venice located in Limbo. And the voice of the barcaiolo asking to be paid at the turning of a canal was left with no response as if face to face with death.

And all the while in my sadness I was happy to feel that you are, Belle. I am happy to have given myself fearlessly to your beauty the way a bird hurls itself into space. Happy, Dear, to have walked, true believers, on the waters of our incertitude as far as that island that is your heart, where suffering grows. Finally: glad.

Rilke, Letter to Mimi Romanelli

My dear Rilke,

"There is death in life and it astonishes me that people pretend not to know that: death whose pitiless presence we feel in each change we survive, for one must learn how to die slowly. We must learn how to die: all our life."

Revolt.
Disorder.
Exuberance.

Le fait même d'écrire, Change/Seghers, 1985

138

Decomposition.
Dread.
Horror.
Fright.
Terror.

You will not emerge, not from silence nor from immobility.

Then let silent drama move in, *so that*.
Then all at once laughter.
: Power.
: Power: calculated defeat of a defeat.

You will not emerge, not from silence nor from immobility.

Very calm. To be sure we were calm.

To be sure we were calm. I do not want to hear any crying, nor
hear any laughing.
To be sure we *are* calm.

The sharp value of calmness: a blade. A blade? Sharpened,
grinding (unlikely?)

We are on the verge...

Right on the verge of all things: Listening — working —writing.
On the verge.

Just exactly as: "on the verge" of "tears."

A *huge anger*. To be sure we were calm.
A huge disorder.
Nothing answering nothing.
To be sure we were solitary — And good — And violent.
And disordered.
And, to ourselves, two-faced.
I don't want any more.

No more space.

Space. Breath. *This* breath. *Short breath.*

To be sure we were calm. Not another word. No more greatness. "You" remain to "you." Falsely calm.

O Tod.*

(Music: the silence it implies.)
A huge anger. Silence "par excellence." The silence of silence.
Not another word bluntly passes.
And we remain essentially impavid. And yet still living. To be sure we were calm.
Not another word and all the words pass.

"The excess" the "silence." Side by side.

I am afraid.
I forget afraid.
I rejoice.
I am afraid.
The gondola. It consoles me and shocks me. From moment to moment.
I am afraid.
I rejoice.
Above all: "I am not."
I am ashamed to tell you this.
We have not seen the canal. We have not lived the canal.
Nor the light. Nothing.

So how can you rejoice (but you rejoice): nothing.
Nothing — rest — Nothing.
Nothing: for we have lived the gondola and lived and lived even more for we have lived the light. In a manner as peaceful as "perfect."

---

*Brahms, *Four Serious Songs.*

Nothing adding to nothing: language.

To be sure we were calm: decomposition itself. Everything came to us, then absolutely from such an absence. From *such* an absence, but from a shy absence.

Shy? And yet it's you who speaks.

Very calm. To be sure we were calm.

"I am not ashamed, Dear, to have wept, another Sunday, cold and too early, in the gondola that kept turning and turning, passing vaguely outlined neighborhoods that seemed to me to belong to another Venice located in Limbo. And the voice of the barcaiolo asking to be paid at the turning of a canal was left with no response as if face to face with death."

We admit without knowing it that the gondola turns and turns. Strange sign of friendship: your tears — *a weary little gesture of the hand*. We admit (admitted?) that the gondola turns and turns, sign to sign. (A weary little gesture of the hand. And of speech.) We admit that the gondola turns
>   And turns
>   And turns

Tears
A vague notion of eternity.
And very exact, precise, death.
Very exact? precise? Death?

Very calm. To be sure we were calm.

The "drama" is here supreme lightness.

The drama?
Nothing escapes laughter. That laughter lighter than light. Light, light to bear in it this word: light.

Thus even lighter.

Sometimes we feel we are sitting in very comfortable armchairs. And heavy. Then gondola and tears come to touch us with their beaks.

You know we are far from you — "there is death in life and it astonishes me that people can not know" — far from you — and near all the dread of nearness.

(At the arm pulse and between the shoulders — vital points — death rebounded.)

"Death itself." "Your own death."

We did not know how to distinguish nearness and distance.

Very calm. To be sure we were calm.

"Drama:" the Grand Canal.
So let move in. Let be. Let the evanescent evanesce.

We had to assume our absence like an increase of language, like a presence: our "own presence."

Absence.
Absence, from flight point to flight point, on a road (rail) one could not define.

And at the same time, as you know, I will speak and speak no more.
I will speak.

"And all the while in my sadness, I am happy to feel that you are, Belle..."

I will speak.

142

You look for the meaning of the word: equivalence.

A deep anger. Peace: alternation.
The here from the here. Equivalence? No, not enough divergence.

You will be you. You will be not.
You will be you. You will be not.

Very calm. To be sure we were calm.

Your tears were but an almost (almost streaming everywhere).
We will be not.
Not, driven from that complacency the sentence is.
Driven. And talking in sentences. Endlessly.

"I am not ashamed to have wept."

This point of vulnerability we take to be inside you, inside us.
Vulnerable?
— Talking — but talking in the fragility of the unlikely.

"And the voice of the barcaiolo asking to be paid at the turning
of the canal went without an answer as if face to face with death."

Fragility is eternity.
How relentlessly we said: yes.
How relentlessly we said: no.

Other and other language.
Must. Will have to. Following you at close range between your
shoulders.

Other and other language.

A point (of peace) will have to be established

This peace.
Peace *so that*.

Claude Royet-Journoud

Letter from Symi

The "Letter from Symi" is an actual letter : I received it by ordinary mail on July 27, 1979. I am quite sure Claude Royet-Journoud never thought this letter, or rather this notebook, would one day become a text. I am writing this note to testify that the idea of publishing this letter is entirely mine, but why exactly make such a proposal to Claude Royet-Journoud, in other words why make available a piece of private correspondence?

That an author be accountable for everything he writes (personal letters, journals or notebooks not meant for publication), that the separation between the voluntary and involuntary work be less clear than the author thinks, must be conceded. But should we not feel more than discomfort at our admission into the heart of what is to us unknown and perhaps excludes us? I have received numerous letters from Claude Royet-Journoud, they are immensely beautiful, but they concern only himself and me and will remain private. Completely otherwise, I realized quite soon, if not right away, that I could not keep the letter from Greece to myself.

The response is simple. I am not only the recipient, but, by my three last books, the object, of this notebook. As a matter of discretion, I could never have been able to suggest its publication had I not always had the sense that this letter was indeed a letter but also, or perhaps first of all, a text by Claude Royet-Journoud. It turned out this way since by "chance" the friend's hand was not separate from that of the writer. I loved the clarity, the violence, the brevity, the vividness, the precision of this prose, frequently broken off, which also renders blank space visible, silence audible, which lets a presence be felt but of what? What wandering fear?   Roger Laporte

Lettre de Symi, Fata Morgana, 1980

LETTER FROM SYMI

18 May

Dear Roger,

There was, first of all, a storm. A storm of wild violence, transforming roads into sheets of water and making the sea earthcolored. Intermittent hail. And, other violence, within this earth : your books. Fascinated by *Suite,* I chose to begin with the *Notebooks*! A way of circling around. Of waiting. And of being with you, in the familiarity of the air, the lines. Of following you with the light touch of friendship. (Of entering passionately.) A thousand remarks come to mind.

. At a certain time you could have written an admirable text on Jaccottet! If I am not mistaken, you have never done that. And that's *impossible* now. I mean, you understand me, your work since *Fugue* has made that text impossible to write...

. On the other hand, certain works of Lars Fredrikson will always be generative (no surprise that you reached Giroux through one of his sculptures). (Want to reread that text of yours.) The whole problem of the nature of transparency as reversed in L.F. Not *transparency* but *reflection*! Shattered identity. Dismemberment. "Sexualization" of space (this is quick but not completely random. I feel something here.)

. Magnificent pages (Daudet/Verne) that sometimes make one miss the autobiographical notation, as Jacqueline puts it, set aside. Whence one comes to imagine that autobiography for you would still be *biography*. Elements of biography.

. Extraordinary "moment" in pages 256-257-258-259... (Importance, among others, of a sentence like "I would like to write so that the critic could not simply *forget* my work" p. 261.)

(Night replaces the storm ; I'm going out. I'm leaving *Notebooks* upon the blue of my table. Face down, open at that page 261. I'm leaving my "monastery"...)

. the welcome

. (p. 94) ...composition in suspense

. *Intensity* of the whole last section of the *Notebooks* (Importance of the "reprises")

. the leap. genre

. Very lovely two-year interruption (1967-1969): what an awakening! (Eskimo art)

("What language can say is only what can be represented to us equally by other means. That everything flows must be expressed in the *application* of language. And if one says that only *present experience* has reality, the word "present" is already super-fluous." L. Wittgenstein)

I am completely rereading *Souvenir de Reims et autres récits.*
("Also, during the whole first movement, instead of hearing the music, I was able simply to see the musician.")
Souvenir de Reims already grasps the thread of the trail (*A migration,* in a sense, is opposed to it.)

The sun is coming back. The house opens up. Voices drop their fear. It's nothing. A day among books. Something blue. A wall. Objects. This hand in the void

Loss already. Body as forgetting. A landscape.
That is, *for nothing.*

My stay doesn't take me from you.

146

Like an arrow.
Which is the one pursued by loss?
Air bruits meaning.
Repetition is without place. Its wandering grounds it. Invisibly, of course.
("Pursue.")
The astonishing possibility, in spite of everything, of a subject ("I" exposed, "I" doubling the play of a fiction, of a speaking-subject). Tearing. "...There is 'something else' only found by writing, a unique, irreplaceable experience that begins only in the moment of writing; if I put so much time into writing, *it's because there is nothing already lived before.*

Preparation of the body, of the hand, of sleeping. In the "uncompletable" act. Always.

"I must recognize that I wanted to introduce a new definition of the book." Joë Bosquet.

" I should never have seen myself in my death mask."

Rereading the first sequence, I'm astonished to think — oddly, at the word *anger* — that there is "lyricism" there. A disturbing lyricism.

Despair. "...a living being who tries to pass as a ventriloquist's dummy." ("Truth.")

Our single movement: a series of figures outside memory.

This is already long ago, but Mathieu B.'s reading bothered me. Today I see he was right! He was able to read further (or *elsewhere, off to the side,* and without any reduction). To revive Jules Verne in Roger Laporte, this is no small thing! It reverses writing, provokes a kind of *metaphoric entropy.* From that perspective, for the fun of it, I'm rereading the first sentence of the second sequence:

> "Prisoner of a whirlpool, of a closed but unbound space, how would I not want to break the circuit!"

There, the metaphoric entropy is at its fullest. It functions in every sense. It overturns any mental grasp. It remains — and will remain — active, *living*.
(or, further on: "Just when I was overtaken with paralysis, on the brink of suffocating etc.")

.

"...I was returning from an accident that had not happened..."
The color of limits.
To give breath to space.
Incantation. (initiatic detour!)
Split within the same thunders.

The nicest and most paradoxical compliment to address to you — also the most outrageous — would be this one: *You are not writing!*
(And wanting to say something quite different — and so much more violent — than: you are written...)

The words of your "undertaking" are they not *the words of love* : passion, suffocation, combat, waiting, whirlpool, prisoner, secret, wound, torture, crisis, misery, destitution, laceration, shipwreck, oath, desire, dizzying slide, attraction and terror, sanctuary, hope, truth, sacrifice, test, faithfulness, deception, to perjure, to keep one's word, pain, mortification, to love, illusion, disillusion, suffering, to break the circuit, heart, fear, agony, torment, safety, happiness, promise, plummet, to be engulfed, adventure, password, painful petrification, to hope, luck, resolution, to disavow, celebration, deliverance, joy, pact, resurrection...

to write, back to the wall
"The question of language, does it constitute the blind spot of my whole undertaking?"

All the world's movement concentrated in a single invisible
point...
"An immobile oscillation."
Suite, Kafka's last book.

"In this moment of calm, of friendship, who is keeping watch?"
Readers still to come

Roger, these pages *light*, and *rapid*
                    to tell you my friendship

                        love,
                                        Claude.

"To write a book is to make the reader present to every vicissi-
tude of a situation one brings to light." Joë Bousquet.

Bio-Bibliographical Notes

Anne-Marie Albiach
b. 1937
Co-editor of the journal *Siècle à mains*. Translator, notably of Zukofsky's "A 9." Among her books are *Flammigère* (1967), *Etat* (1971), *Mezza Voce* (1984), *Anawratha*(1984) and *«Figure vocative»* (1985).

In English:
«Vocative Figure» (trans. Anthony Barnett & Joseph Simas), Moving
    Letters, 1986
Mezza Voce (trans. Joseph Simas, with Anthony Barnett, Lydia
    Davis & Douglas Oliver), Post-Apollo Press, 1988
Etat (trans. K. Waldrop), Awede Press, 1989
A Geometry (trans. K. & R. Waldrop), Burning Deck: "Série
    d'Ecriture," 1998

Joë Bousquet
1897-1950
Bousquet, his adult life determined by a paralyzing wound to the spinal column received a few months before the end of WWI, was extremely active as a writer and involved with literary movements and journals such as *Cahiers du Sud*. His many books include *Langage entier, La neige d'un autre âge* and a vast published correspondence.

Danielle Collobert
1940-1978
Born into a Breton family active in the Resistance during the Second World War, Collobert moved to Paris at the age of 19. Her journals (forthcoming in translation from Meow Press) track

her engagement with writing as well as her involvement with the FLN during Algeria's struggle for independence. Her books are *Meurtre* (1964), *Dire I-II* (1972), *Il donc* (1976) and her final work, *Survie* (1978).*fæ*

In English:
It Then (trans. Norma Cole), O Books, 1989

Edith Dahan
b. 1940
Epoques pour la guerre (1984)

Jean Daive
b. 1941
Editor of the magazines *fragment* (1970-72), *fig.* (1989-92) and *FIN* (1999-), translator of Paul Celan, Robert Creeley and others. Some titles of Daive's own books are *Décimale blanche* (1967), *Fut bâti* (1973), *N,M,U* (1975), *Un transitif* (1984), *Narration d'équilibre* (4 vols., 1982-1990), *La Condition d'infini* (4 vols., 1995-1997). Daive is also an extraordinary photographer.

In English:
White Decimal (trans. Cid Corman), Origin, 1969
A Lesson in Music (trans. Julie Kalendek), Burning Deck: "Série d'Ecriture," 1992

André du Bouchet
b. 1924
Author of many books of poetry, including *Dans la chaleur vacante* (1961), *Qui n'est pas tourné vers nous* (1972), *L'incohérence* (1979) and *Cendre tirant sur le bleu* (1991). He translated Celan, Mandelstam and Shakespeare, and wrote on Baudelaire, Hölderlin, and Giacometti, among others.

In English:
The Uninhabited (trans. Paul Auster), Living Hand, 1976; reprinted in Paul Auster, *Translations,* Marsilio Publishers, 1997
Where Heat Looms (trans. David Mus), Sun & Moon, 1996

Dominique Fourcade

b. 1937

Winner of the Prix national de la Poésie, some of his many books are *Le ciel pas d'angle* (1983), *Rose-déclic* (1984), *Son blanc du un* (1986), *Xbo* (1988), *Outrance utterance et autres élégies* (1990), *Au travail ma chérie,* illustrated by Pierrre Buraglio (1992), *Décisions ocres* (1992), *iL* (1994), *Le sujet monotype* (1997) and *é té après avoir écrit Le sujet monotype,* with Pierre Buraglio (1997).

In English:

Xbo (trans. Robert Kocik), Sun & Moon, 1993

Click-Rose (trans. Keith Waldrop), Sun & Moon, 1996

Liliane Giraudon

b. 1946

On the editorial board of *Action poétique* for several years, and cofounder (with Jean-Jacques Viton) of the innovative literary journal *Banana Split.* Giraudon's books include *Têtes ravagées : un fresque* (1979), *Je marche ou je m'endors* (1982), *Divagation des chiens* (1988), *Pallaksch, Pallaksch* (Prix Maupassant, 1990) and *Fur* (1992).

In English:

Pallaksch, Pallaksch (trans. Julia Hine), Sun & Moon, 1994

Fur (trans. Guy Bennett), Sun & Moon, 1995

Joseph Guglielmi

b. 1929

Translator of Cole, Corman, Coolidge, Eigner, Spicer (*Billy the Kid*), Rosmarie Waldrop and others, Guglielmi is the author of essays and of many works of poetry, among which are *Aube* (1968), *Le mais trop blanc* (1977), *La préparation des titres* (1980), *Fins de vers* (1986), *Das, la mort* (1987), *Joe's bunker* (1991), *K ou Le dit du passage* (1992), *Grungy Project* (1997) and most recently *Travelogue* (2000).

In English:

Dawn (trans. Rosmarie Waldrop), Spectacular Diseases: "Série d'Ecriture," 1991

Emmanuel Hocquard

b. 1940

Director, with Raquel, of Orange Export Ltd., curator of the poetry reading series at l'ARC, founder of Le Bureau sur l'Atlantique, major contributor to the Royaumont translation seminars and collector of Depression glass, Hocquard co-edited (with Claude Royet-Journoud) *21+1 poètes américains d'aujourd'hui* (1986) and *49 + 1 nouveaux poètes américains* (1991). His writings include *Album d'images de la Villa Harris* (1978), *Une journée dans le détroit* (1980), *Aerea dans les forêts de Manhattan* (1985), *Un privé à Tanger* (1987), *Théorie des Tables* (1992), *Le Commanditaire* (with Juliette Valéry,1993) and *Un test de solitude : sonnets* (1998).

In English:

A Day in the Straits (trans. Maryann DeJulio & Jean Staw), Red Dust, 1984

Late Additions (trans. Rosmarie Waldrop & Connell McGrath), Spectacular Diseases: "Série d'Ecriture," 1988

Elegies & Other Poems (trans. John A. Scott), Shearsman Books, 1989

Theory of Tables (trans. Michael Palmer), O.blek Editions, 1994

Aerea in the Forests of Manhattan (Prix France-Culture, trans. Lydia Davis), Marlboro, 1994

This Story is Mine (trans. Norma Cole), Instress, 1998

A Test of Solitude (trans. Rosmarie Waldrop), Burning Deck: "Série d'Ecriture," 2000

Codicil (trans. Ray DiPalma and Juliette Valéry), Post-Apollo Press, 2000

Roger Laporte

b. 1925

Laporte's relentless exploration of life/writing/life appeared in *Une vie : biographie* (1986), collecting previously published volumes among which *La veille* (1963), *Une voix de fin silence* (1966), *Pourquoi?* (1967), *Fugue* (1970), *Supplément* (1973), *Suite* (1979) and *Moriendo* (1983). Some of his other books are *Lettre à personne: Carnets,* with an Introduction by Lacoue-Labarthe and a Postface by Maurice Blanchot (1989), *A l'extreme pointe : Proust, Bataille, Blanchot* (1998) and *La loi de l'alternance,* essays on Rilke, Van Gogh and Mozart (1997).

Roger Lewinter
b. 1941
Among Lewinter's writings are *Groddeck et le Royaume millénaire de Jérome Bosch* (1974), *Diderot ou les mots de l'absence* (1976), *L'Attrait des choses* (1985), *Histoire de l'amour dans la solitude* (1989) and *qui –dans l'ordre –au rouge du soir –des mots-* (1998). This last text, magnificent, was meant to appear in *Crosscut Universe*, but was revoked upon Lewinter's decision to rewrite it.

Raquel
The painter Raquel does not include a bio note for herself in *Orange Export Ltd. 1969-1986*, the anthology of the important publishing project she and Emmanuel Hocquard co-directed. A force in the history of small press publishing in France, Raquel, also a writer and scholar, has collaborated with many other writers as a visual artist. She currently publishes *Notes*.

Mitsou Ronat
Linguist, writer, theorist, part of the *Change* collective and contributor to *Action poétique* and Orange Export Ltd.

Jacques Roubaud
b. 1932
Mathematician, member of Oulipo, translator of Jack Spicer and others, member of the editorial committees of *Action poétique*, *Change*, and *Po&sie*, esteemed authority on the Troubador poets, writer of works of all genres, among his books are *E* (1967), *Mono no aware : le sentiment des choses* (1970), *Renga* (with Octavio Paz, Edouardo Sanguinetti and Charles Tomlinson, 1971), *Trente et un au cube* (1973), *Mezura* (1975), *Graal fiction* (1978), *Les troubadours* (1981), *Quelque chose noir* (1986), *La fleur inverse* (1986), *Le grand incendie de Londres* (1989), *La pluralité des mondes de Lewis* (1991), *La Boucle* (1993), *L'Invention du fils de Léoprepes* (1994), *Poésie etcetera : ménage* (1995), *la fenêtre veuve* (1996), and *La forme d'une ville change plus vite, hélas, que le coeur des humains* (1999).

In English:
Some Thing Black (trans. Rosmarie Waldrop), Dalkey Archive, 1990

The Plurality of Worlds of Lewis (trans. Rosmarie Waldrop), Dalkey Archive, 1995

The Great Fire of London (trans. Dominic Di Bernardi), Dalkey Archive, 1991

Hortense is Abducted (trans. Dominic Di Bernardi), Dalkey Archive, 1989

Hortense in Exile (trans. Dominic Di Bernardi), Dalkey Archive, 1992

Agnès Rouzier
d. 1981

The work of Agnès Rouzier, *Non, rien,* plus work published in literary journals such as *Change,* as well as her unpublished writing is collected in the volume *Le fait même d'écrire* (1985), also the title of her writing on Blanchot.

Claude Royet-Journoud
b.1941

Editor of *Siècle à mains* (with Anne-Marie Albiach and Michel Couturier), of *21+1 poètes américains d'aujourd'hui* and *49 + 1 nouveaux poètes américains* (with Emmanuel Hocquard), of *zuk* and *l'in-plano,* Royet-Journoud is the author of the tetralogy, *Le renversement* (1972), *La notion d'obstacle* (1978), *Les objets contiennent l'infini* (1983) and *Les natures indivisibles* (1997). His translations of George Oppen appear in the anthology *Vingt poètes américains* (1980). His contributions to poetry, too numerous and complex to document here, have been celebrated in *je te continue ma lecture: Mélanges pour Claude Royet-Journoud* (1999). Royet-Journoud's paintings have been exhibited in Paris and a series of painted photographs, *Laque sur Polaroïd,* was published with a text by Dominique Fourcade, "Compact pour Claude."

In English:

Reversal (trans. Keith Waldrop), Hellcoal, 1973

The Notion of Obstacle (trans. Keith Waldrop), Awede, 1985

The Maternal Drape (trans. Charles Bernstein), Awede, 1985

Objects Contain the Infinite (trans. Keith Waldrop), Awede, 1995

A Descriptive Method (trans. Keith Waldrop), Post-Apollo, 1995

i.e. (trans. Keith Waldrop), Burning Deck: "Série d'Ecriture," 1995

Norma Cole

is a poet, painter and translator. Her most recent poetry publications are *The Vulgar Tongue* (a+bend press, 2000), *Desire & Its Double* (Instress, 1998) and *Spinoza in Her Youth* (A.bacus, February 1999). *Scout*, a text/image work, is forthcoming from Krupskaya Editions in CD-ROM format. Her current translation work includes Danielle Collobert's *Journals*, Anne Portugal's *Nude* and a book of poetry by Lebanese writer Fouad Gabriel Naffah. Cole has been the recipient of a Wallace Alexander Gerbode Foundation Award, Gertrude Stein Awards, as well as awards from The Fund for Poetry. Canadian by birth, Cole migrated via France to San Francisco where she has lived for over twenty years.

For more information about available translations:

A most useful and unique source is *A Selective Bibliography of French Poetry in Translation Published in Small Press Journals from 1980-1992*, compiled by Alan Gilbert and Kristin Prevallet, 1995. The bibliography can be obtained by request from Gilbert and Prevallet, 23 Greenpoint Ave., Brooklyn NY 11222.

(One hopes for someone to undertake the sequel covering the period, nearly a decade, from 1992 to the present.)

In 1994, Small Press Distribution published a catalogue of works in translation. This information is constantly being updated. These books and journals may be ordered directly through orders@spdbooks.org OR by calling 1-800-869-7553 or, in the Bay Area, 510-524-1668 OR by writing to Small Press Distribution, 1341 Seventh Street, Berkeley CA 94710.

And see the website durationpress.com through which Burning Deck and many other sources (publishers and websites) may be accessed.

Série d'Ecriture

No. 1: Alain Veinstein, *Archeology of the Mother* (trans. Tod Kabza, Rosmarie Waldrop), 1986

No. 2: Emmanuel Hocquard, *Late Additions* (trans. Connell McGrath, Rosmarie Waldrop), 1988

No. 3: Anne-Marie Albiach, Marcel Cohen, Jean Daive, Dominique Fourcade, Jean Frémon, Paol Keineg, Jacqueline Risset, Jacques Roubaud, Claude Royet-Journoud (trans. Anthony Barnett, Charles Bernstein, Lydia Davis, Serge Gavronsky, Rachel Stella, Keith Waldrop, Rosmarie Waldrop), 1989

No. 4: Anne-Marie Albiach, Olivier Cadiot, Danielle Collobert, Edith Dahan, Serge Fauchereau, Dominique Fourcade, Liliane Giraudon, Joseph Guglielmi, Vera Linhartova, Anne Portugal (trans. Charles Bernstein, Norma Cole, Robert Kocik, Natasha, Ron Padgett, Keith Waldrop, Rosmarie Waldrop), 1990

No. 5: Joseph Guglielmi, *Dawn* (trans. Rosmarie Waldrop), 1991

No. 6: Jean Daive, *A Lesson in Music* (trans. Julie Kalendek), 1992

No. 7: Pierre Alferi, Jean-Pierre Boyer, Olivier Cadiot, Dominique Fourcade, Jean Frémon, Jean-Marie Gleize, Dominique Grandmont, Emmanuel Hocquard, Isabelle Hovald, Anne Portugal, Jacques Roubaud, James Sacré, Anne Talvaz, Esther Tellerman (trans. David Ball, Norma Cole, Stacy Doris, Paul Green, Tom Mandel, Pam Rehm, Cole Swensen, Keith Waldrop, Rosmarie Waldrop), 1993

No. 8: Paol Keineg, *Boudica* (trans. Keith Waldrop), 1994

No. 9: Marcel Cohen, *The Peacock Emperor Moth* (trans. Cid Corman), 1995

No. 10: Jacqueline Risset, *The Translation Begins* (trans. Jennifer Moxley), 1996

No. 11: Alain Veinstein, *Even a Child* (trans. Robert Kocik, Rosmarie Waldrop), 1997

No. 12: Emmanuel Hocquard, *A Test of Solitude* (trans. Rosmarie Waldrop), 2000

No. 13/14: *Crosscut Universe: Writing on Writing from France* (ed./trans. Norma Cole) 2000

Supplements:

No. 1: Claude Royet-Journoud, *i.e.* (trans. Keith Waldrop), 1995

No. 2: Pascal Quignard, *Sarx* (trans. Keith Waldrop), 1997

No. 3: Anne-Marie Albiach, *A Geometry* (trans. Keith Waldrop, Rosmarie Waldrop), 1998